CHASING
SUCCESS

Dr. Alok Trivedi

Chasing Success

Dr. Alok Trivedi

Copyright © 2017 by Dash Enterprises & Dr. Alok Trivedi
Author Dr. Alok Trivedi
Published by Dash Enterprises
Book Design by Red Raven Book Design

Chasing Success
(publisher Dash)
ISBN 978-0-9989269-0-2
Website: Draloktrivedi.com

DR. ALOK TRIVEDI

Acknowledgements

This book is the culmination of many years of work effort and dedication; not mine, rather my parents. You two are the rock behind the source of this book that was just an idea many years ago, but because of your support it is now a reality.

To Daiven—my mini-me—this book is dedicated to the light I see in you and who you are. You are not only an inspiration, but true motivation for me and the rest of the world.

To Ashianna—my biggest fan—I will dedicate a message to you that only you will understand. "If one child believes…" you know the rest of it. It's your constant faith and belief in me that has driven me to create this book.

To all the people I have not mentioned, who have unconditionally supported and to those who challenged, I thank you because through both I got to experience love.

Sincerely,
Dr. Alok Trivedi

DR. ALOK TRIVEDI

Introduction

To the reader,

My obsession for understanding life began at the age of five. Growing up in an East Indian home I found my identity through Eastern ways of thought. Living in Toronto, Canada, I saw myself through the lens of the traditions and values that were driven from a country so far away.

As I grew older I saw that life didn't have to be that way and there was a different way of thinking. I began to see the world from a different vantage point, almost to the point that I began to negate my previous self as many people do in today's society.

It wasn't until I began to see the world from both philosophical positions that I began to really understand who I was—a merger of worlds and life without barriers, and more importantly a life without labels.

The idea of Chasing Success came as I saw people in the East constantly searching for this everlasting nirvana and spirituality. It seemed that the greater their dedication to spirituality, the further they perceived themselves to be successful; until it became an obsession to find greater levels of so called peace. For many, this equaled a successful life.

Where in the West, the idea of materialism and a fast-paced world created success. Materialism, more money, more power, and more success equaled a successful life. Yet for many, including celebrities, this leads to chaos and destruction of their lives.

Where is the success in either of these vantage points? It wasn't until I saw the world through both lenses when things began to make sense. This book can be classified as a personal leadership book—a performance book. I tend to consider it a book to help you achieve alignment, which to me is about finding yourself and living and performing from that state.

I hope that you find this book enjoyable and that it allows you to think about things a little differently than you did before reading it. It is my humble request that you honor yourself, because only then will you impact the world.

Chapter One

"Death is not the greatest loss in life. The greatest loss is what dies inside us while we live."
– Norman Cousins

"If you were to die tomorrow, how would you spend today?" He had asked, not too long ago. The question rolled over in my mind as I gazed down at the coffin. I didn't have an answer for him then, and I still didn't, standing at his funeral and far too late to give my answer. The acrid smell of incense settled in the temple, burning my throat.

"I'm so sorry, Shah," I whispered, unable to stop the tear tracking its way slowly down my cheek. The crush of people waiting for their moment behind me made me feel foolish; I thought he would be alone in the end, when I received notice of his funeral a few days before. I felt sure that I would be the lone representative, holding a prayer over him as he was laid to rest. His life as a park vendor did not, after all, lead to greatness. With tentative fingers I touched the edge of his coffin, overcome by how little I knew about him.

Sighing, I whispered, "I thought being here would somehow be enough."

Arriving at the temple moments ago, I found myself faced with an unexpected throng of people. My black suit jacket made me feel much more out of place than I realized alongside the other mourners wearing the traditional white clothing befitting this kind of funeral. I considered turning back, vanishing without a backward glance. But Shah had meant more to me than to justify that behavior. I had to push my way into the building, garnering more than a few angry glares. But I made my way through, and there I was, insistent upon paying my last respects. The words of our final conversation played over again in my mind.

"Because if you live your days in any way other than how you would choose to spend your last, then you do not live for yourself." He had laughed, as he poured the tea.

"I don't understand that," I said reaching for the tea. "Not even a little bit, Shah."

Since moving to Chicago, I have not been a part of the community as much as my parents would have wanted me to be. The view, as I walked up the sidewalk, of so many people—none of which knew me—gave me a crashing awareness of how little I actually knew about Shah. To me, he had been nothing more than a park vendor, an extremely wise and self-aware park vendor, but nothing more, nonetheless.

At last, I stepped away from the coffin and allowed the next person to step forward. I joined the outer edges of the crowd, finding myself searching for faces I may recognize. Every eye in the room seemed to bore into me, standing out from the crowd. Not one face appeared of those I had seen with him at the park. No one struck a familiarity, at least not right away. The heady scent of ceremonial incense wafted in a thin, white veil over the crowd.

I recalled the first time I spoke with him. I had seen him in passing countless times, without a glance. He always smiled and handed out treats, a crowd of eager, happy children surrounding him like the Pied Piper. His booth was as much a part of the park as the large trees surrounding the path. I cannot recall exactly when we developed the habit of a friendly wave each time I passed; his wide grin accompanying a toss of his hand my way. I returned this gesture, of course, with a perfunctory nod. Every now and then, I had seen one of the other joggers purchasing an energy drink from him, something he sold alongside the standard offering of kebobs.

Settling in against the wall, hidden by the crowd, I felt hollow inside, empty, a deeper part of me grasping and searching again for that which evaded me. The pang pierces me as my glance landed once more on the deceased. I wondered, should I die, would my expression would be quite as serene as his? There were equal parts of humility, gratitude, and grief wrestling for a place in the hollow cavern inside my chest.

A few of the inhabitants turned towards me with some curiosity. My choice of dress was so unlike theirs. I am a black clad American in a sea of tradition. Leaning against the side wall to watch the remainder of the ceremony, I could see the Pujari over the heads of the reverent gathered, placing the ornaments alongside the body and wafting the incense over the upturned, silent faces. I felt more alone than I ever had in a long while.

"They are not doing a cremation," I heard spoken close by from one woman to another. "The family wishes to have him interred at the cemetery."

"That is rare," the other woman replied.

The crowd began to move around and low voices broke the silence, marking the end of the ceremony. I felt puzzled at the presence of those around me, once more experiencing a bit of ownership over the man. *It makes no sense,* I thought, *that he would be surrounded by these people, none of which I had heard him mention during our many discussions.* I pushed my way towards the two women.

"Excuse me," I interrupted. "Where will they bury him?"

They both turned and faced me with raised eyebrows, taken aback most likely, by my brusk approach. It was not intended, but my desire for knowledge outweighed my ability to maintain a politeness appropriate to the occasion.

"Where?" I asked again. "Where will they take his body?"

A young man I had never seen before, made his way towards me through the crowd. I remained facing him, keeping our eyes locked and acknowledging that it is me he is seeking. The broad shoulders and firm step created a sense of ownership and dominance. I matched his position, with the slight adjustment of tilting back my shoulders.

"You were asking questions about Mr. Naahn?" he said, after arriving within earshot. His speech was relaxed but his gaze remained steady.

"Yes, I was," I replied placing my hand over my heart and flicking my gaze towards the woman standing behind him. "I did not mean to upset anyone. Perhaps the emotion of the day affected my intention. I merely wanted to know where I could go to pay my respects in the future."

"Who are you," he demanded. "Why are you here?"

"I'm a friend of Shah's," I insisted. Surely I had been mentioned to this man, whoever he might be.

"How do you know him?" His brow furrowed and his eyes blazed.

"He's the park vendor. I used to meet with him!" The intensity in my voice attracted a few more glances in the still reverent crowd milling around us. I ignored them, focusing on the upstart before me. "Who do you think you are?"

"I'm his son!"

The young man drew up his posture. Once more I was overcome with the realization of how little I knew about my old mentor. What an insignificant part of his life I must have been, after all. All this time I thought I had known Shah, I had thought of myself as the greater of the two of us, that I was reaching from my position in life to one of the lower caste. This uniquely American idea—that we could all be aligned equally—had me thinking that I had somehow elevated him with my presence in his humble life. With a slow and painful dawning, I realized how much of this had been arrogance on my part.

Earlier in the week, the day I found out about his death, the hollow feeling in my chest did nothing for my frame of mind.

My wife, Nikki, came to mind. Ex-wife now, I guess. For a brief moment, I considered calling her, already knowing this would not be a good idea. There was really no point in going there. I turned on my computer before heading to the kitchen for a protein shake.

There was no one to call.

Flipping through the names in my phone, I realized that every name there was someone from work, older numbers, including the people we used to spend time with before the divorce; our "couple-friends", as my wife called them. Most of them had veered out of my life over the last year. Nothing intentional, of course. It always starts with the wide-eyed "Let's get together sometime soon."

And then, maybe even if the offer is taken. Showing up to the dinner party, only after careful deliberation on whether or not *she* might be there ("Not this time. She sends her regrets," they say). You sit there, watching all the couples around you, realizing that without that common glue to hold down the awkward conversation, your wife's friends are just that—your wife's friends.

And then a couple more weeks go by and maybe you run into them in the grocery store. They smile, forcing the expression into their eyes. You smile back. Idle chit chat, and then "Let's get together sometime soon." This time, both knowing you are just reciting lines and playing the part. And just like that, we walk out of each other's lives as easily as stepping across the sensors to the automatic doors into the oppressive heat of the grocery store parking lot.

I had no one to call.

I wondered if I only went to the funeral to sooth my own wounded ego, instead of doing it for him. I fully expected no one to be there. Maybe a few stragglers from the park. I could not have been more wrong.

Chapter Two
Three Years Prior

"There is no easy walk to freedom anywhere, and many of us will have to pass through the valley of the shadow of death again and again before we reach the mountaintop of our desires."
– Nelson Mandela

"You've got to come with us," boomed Frank Benjamin, company President, as he clapped me on the shoulder with his broad hand. Everyone else filtered out of the board room, chatting and smiling as the meeting came to an end.

In my pocket, my cell phone buzzed and I knew it was my wife calling.

"Tonight might not be good for me," I replied.

"What's going on?" Dave popped up next to us with his typical smiling, eager expression. I had just received a nod of consideration for the VP slot, which usually included an outing with higher ups, lots of kissing up, and a late-night home to an angry spouse.

"Our boy here is dragging his feet about celebrating his big step up in life," Benjamin bellowed with a hefty chortle. Dave rolled his eyes, matching our boss's demeanor and mood.

"Oh, come on, Kumar! You're the man of the hour. You have to come out with us." And just like that, Dave managed to get himself invited, almost without anyone else noticing him doing so. He had been sniffing at my boot heels for years. I found it par for the course.

"So what's it going to be, then? Sushi or lobster?" Benjamin asked with an affable grin.

"Gentlemen," I replied, holding the still-buzzing phone between us. "If you will excuse me. I need to take this."

I stepped into the hallway and answered.

"What time will you be home?" The still voice of my wife asked on the other end.

"I don't know if I'll make it by dinner. Benjamin wants me to go out to celebrate."

"Celebrate what?" The slight tremor, only detectable by someone who knew it well, indicated her unhappiness.

"That's the good news at least. I'm on the short list for the VP slot."

"I thought you said you would take your name out of consideration for that."

"I know, I know, Nikki. I did say that."

"So what changed?"

Good question. The truth was, I still wanted it. Having joined Green Point as a salesman fresh out of college, I considered it my obligation to work my way up, schmoozing and rubbing elbows at company picnics. Frank Benjamin had noticed my numbers, taken me in under his wing early in the game, and readied the path for me. I didn't just get lucky. I had earned this. She had to understand. I earned it. I deserved it.

"You didn't tell them. Did you?" she demanded.

"Nikki, you know this would look good for me. This would change a lot for us if I got chosen for it. I'm doing this for you and the kids. You know that."

"The kids need you here. They don't care one bit how much money you are making. They just want their dad home for dinner, Kumar. They need you. I need you too."

"I can't say no to this Nikki. It would look good for me to do a little bit of schmoozing."

"Fine. You're right. This would be good for us, I guess. I'll figure out something to tell the kids. They'll be disappointed, but I am sure they'll understand. I'll see you when you get home. I love you."

"I love you too, Nikki."

A faint click and she was gone. I turned towards the men exiting the meeting room and tried to add some sincerity to the smile on my face. I had the privilege of joining the merry men on one of their promotion outings before, and I wondered how much Benjamin was motivated by his desire to eat expensive meals and drinks on the company dime. Every time someone made partner or got a promotion within the higher levels it was the same old song and dance.

Within the hour, I found myself sitting in front of an expansive table of sushi, ranging from Maki rolls to expertly sliced sashimi, scrolling by on the lazy conveyer belt. The phone call with Nikki had left a bad taste in my mouth, but Benjamin pushed the Sake towards me with a knowing grin and slowly, any lingering misgivings were erased.

"I'm liking you, Kumar," he told me, as he gave me a strong pat on the back. "It's pretty remarkable what you have managed to pull off during your time at the company."

"Do you think so?" I said with a grin.

"Are you kidding?" His boisterous laugh gathered glances from nearby tables. "Going from the sales floor to sitting at the edge of VP in three short years? I'd say that's pretty remarkable."

The night stretched out before me. Plates came and went, serving up to us the formidable delicacies created by the white-clad sushi chef standing before us. I found myself pushing the idea of Nikki out of my mind, justifying the path that appeared before me. I could've called her to come get me. I could've called a taxi. I could've grabbed Dave and talked him into ducking out with me, but none of those felt like the right thing to do. I was, after all, indebted to Benjamin—the President of the company. If I wanted my life to change, I had to stay on his good side.

"What do you do?" an attractive woman nearby asked, as she stroked her painted fingertips up and down the plastic stir straw.

"Vice President at Green Point," I replied. It was almost true, at least.

Dave, Benjamin and I had moved to a bar—a dimly lit, low key room filled with modern sculptures and smiling movie posters. The perfumed lady, with glossy lips and smoky eyes, had made her way over, perched next to me and leaned in, close enough that the curve of her shoulder pressed against my arm. Her rapt attention felt pretty good, if I were to admit the truth to myself. I couldn't help it. Her heavily mascaraed eyes looked at me in a way which Nikki had not in a long time and it sparked something in me.

"Ooh," she purred. Her eyes narrowed and she stroked the smooth surface of the bar with her lacquered nails. "That sounds fascinating."

Dave returned to the table, slid in next to the girl by me, casted a wicked grin my way, and patted me on the shoulder.

The phone buzzed again, but I ignored it. The call could go to voice mail.

Chapter Three

"True greatness consists in being great in little things."
– Charles Simmons

The morning came and went without much more discussion. I walked through my day in a fog, only partially brought on by the previous night out. Nikki had managed to avoid me for the duration of the morning, her ambivalence masked by the hustle and bustle of getting the kids fed, ready for school and out the door. She gave me a frosty glare but snapped towards me the perfunctory "Love you!" before vanishing out the door.

Work crept by, minute by minute.

"Here man," Dave said, appearing at my door with a Gatorade.

"Thanks."

He sat down in the chair across from my desk, and I swung away from the computer screen, rubbing my thumbs against my temples.

"Anything important?" he asked.

"Finance reports. So, no." I cracked the seal of the drink and tilted it back, the cool bitter liquid doing much too little to pacify my headache.

"Man, that was some serious celebrating last night," Dave exclaimed. "You must be a shoe in for that VP slot."

"I guess so." In retrospect, the whole scene struck me as ridiculous. The falseness of the exchange between the dull eyed bar patrons. Maybe it had been the expression on Dave's face, the maniacal grin and leering side glances, making whatever assumptions he was capable of. I downed my drink and tossed the empty bottle into the can behind my desk.

"You know what, Dave," I said, standing and picking up my jacket off the back of my chair. "I think I'm going to knock out early."

"Hey, yeah. Okay." He stood and slowly stepped out of my office. He looked a bit disappointed that I had not picked up the bait about whatever it was he had wanted to talk about. All I wanted to do was to get out and get some fresh air. On most days, I could handle Dave and his annoyances, but not today.

"Oh, hey!" Dave called out to me as I brushed past him into the hallway. "I almost forgot to tell you. Benjamin wants you to come by his office."

"Alright, thanks," I replied out loud, while I thought to myself, *great.*

I hung a right towards the boss's corner office and walked through the large, glass double doors leading into the entryway where his secretary sat, a plump lady with a modest low bun and an easy smile.

"Oh, Hello Kumar," she said as I entered.

"How are you, Cynthia?" I asked as I offered her a small smile.

"I'll let Mr. Benjamin know you are here." She pressed a few buttons, and moments later, he appeared, holding open one of the oak double doors to his private office, waving me in.

"Come in, my boy, come in!" He looked no worse for the wear. His face held the usual ruddiness and his demeanor appeared large and dominating, as usual. Here was a man who liked to indulge, and may have been already; I caught a faint whiff of gin as I walked passed him. He sat down at his desk and methodically began to unbutton his sleeves with his large fingers. I didn't feel particularly worried, but I nodded and settled in for one of his speeches.

"My boy, I don't want you to worry about this whole VP thing," he said taking his jacket off. "Truth is, you're the best candidate for the position."

"Thank you, sir."

"There is one bit of business that I want you to go through before we make it official. Nothing to worry about. Not even a little bit. But the Board of Directors insists this is just part of the vetting process. Red tape, really. Nothing more."

"What is it, sir?" I asked, growing uneasy as he spoke.

"Take a look at this." He reached across his desk and handed me a business card. "Some of the board members think it might be a good idea if you give this guy a visit."

I examined the stiff paper between my fingers. It contained a name, address and phone number. Nothing more. "Mr. Benjamin. I'm not sure I understand what this is about."

"I suppose," he replied leaning back and lacing his fingers together behind his head. "You could say this guy is kind of a business adviser."

"Do you think that is something I need, sir?" If I were to be honest with myself, it bruised my ego to have this given to me right before this promotion. Why couldn't he just push it through?

"It's not up to me, Kumar. The board needs it done. I don't know what it's about, but the guy's supposed to give you some kind of sign off. It sounds like a bunch of nonsense to me, but apparently this guy has helped a couple of them. Just go, get the sign off and you should be good."

Nodding my head and shrugging my shoulders I said, "Thank you, sir."

I tucked the card into my back pocket, waving to Cynthia as I exited the office. If I had to call this guy to get the promotion, then that is what I would have to do.

***

"So what does he do, exactly?" Nikki asked, leaning against the kitchen counter after the kids trundled out the door towards the school bus.

"I'm not exactly sure, to be honest, but the board wants me to see him. I'm meeting him at the park at eleven. That's what he said when I called him yesterday." I reached around her to grab the coffee pot.

"Oh, here," she said, as she handed me my travel mug. "I already made your cup for you."

I glanced down at the ceramic mug in my hand and realized my mistake. "I don't deserve you, you know," I said with a smile.

"I know," she returned the smile and leaned in as I kissed her gently on the lips. She smoothed her hands across the fabric of my button up shirt. "But you're going to be late. Go on now."

***

I arrived at the park a few minutes early, pulling up and glancing around to see if I could spot this guy. A young, blonde woman jogged by, her ponytail whipping back and forth with each step. A man in a business suit sat at one of the benches, glancing at his watch now and then. I took a few steps towards him. He looked up and smiled but the person behind me, a suited woman, stepped past me and returned his greeting. Okay, that wasn't him. A picnicking family ran by, children brushing past me to find their spot on the grassy expanse. At the far edge, I spotted a man—the park vendor—standing behind a small kebob station. He was cleaning the surface with a white cloth.

"Can we go? Can we, please?" the children from the picnicking family implored their parents.

"Okay, but come right back and don't ruin your appetite."

I watched with some amusement as they ran over to the park vendor. He greeted them with a wide white-toothed smile, handing them each a small toothpick with a morsel of spiced meat on the end. They thanked him and returned to their parents, the smiles on their faces revealing their delight.

Slightly annoyed that my appointment had not yet arrived, I strolled over to the vendor.

"Soda, please," I said, squinting at the cast of dark clouds appearing overhead. He handed me the drink, carefully watching my gaze. Briefly, I considered what may happen to his booth if it rained. Just as I handed him the bills, large fat raindrops began to fall from the sky, spreading and joining together on the pavement. He leaned down, struggling to pull the large umbrella from underneath his stand. The umbrella was huge and cumbersome. I rushed to help him. Together we struggled to get the thing upright, tucking the pole into the hole in the corner of his stand and opening it just in time to guard against the worst of the downpour.

"Thank you," he said nodding his head.

"Of course," I replied.

"You are waiting for someone?"

"Yes. Late for an appointment," I answered, as I glanced around. "I should go. Let you return to your work."

"Who are you waiting for?" he asked before I could escape.

"A business associate." I gave a polite smile, hardly more than a grimace and tried to walk away, quickly enough to escape without appearing rude.

"Mr. Benjamin said you would come," he called out. I stopped and turned slowly to face him.

"How do you know Mr. Benjamin?"

"You are here to meet with Mr. S. Naahn, is that correct?"

"Yes," I replied, aghast.

"At your service," he said extending his hand, introducing himself simply as Shah. The rain fell around us and I realized my suit had gotten quite wet. He stood perfectly dry underneath his large umbrella, still smiling. Unsure of what else to do, I stepped forward, ducking my head under the edge of the covering and took his hand.

"It's nice to meet you," I said. My confusion could not have been greater.

Chapter Four

In all chaos there is a cosmos, in all disorder a secret order.
– Carl Jung

"So just what exactly is it that you do, Shah?" I asked, as we sat in his studio apartment, a humble abode with a small kitchenette in one corner and a teapot rumbling on the stove top.

After the rain continued, he had invited me across the park to step inside his apartment and dry off. I followed, unsure of what I might be in for. Upon stepping inside, he handed me a towel, which I used to dabbed at my face and shoulders. Across the room, he hung my jacket on the back of a wooden chair to dry.

My question had prompted another wry smile. He did not answer right away, but stood and poured us both a cup of tea in two small, plain china cups stained with years of use. The warmth eased my agitation just a bit, but curiosity still plagued me.

"What I do," he replied slowly, lowering into the plush chair across from me "Is sell kebobs in the park."

"Yes," I replied. "But Mr. Benjamin said—"

He raised his hand and shook his head. "What Mr. Benjamin said is of no consequence. He is not here now."

I shifted in my seat and took a sip of tea, mostly out of politeness. The man had closed his eyes, his cup and saucer cradled in his hands. For a moment, I thought he may have fallen asleep and I tensed to leap forward and catch the dishes, which were sure to tumble to the floor at any moment.

"What is the reason for coming here," he asked, his eyes still closed.

"I…I'm not sure. The board of directors wanted me to come."

"That is not correct."

"What?"

"You are here of your own accord. It is you who are sitting here with me. Is that not so?"

"Yes," I stammered. "I guess that is so."

"This board of directors is not here, are they?"

"They are not," I replied, swallowing with some difficulty.

He opened his eyes and glanced my way. If I were not mistaken I could have sworn I saw amusement dancing behind his eyes. "So I ask you again, what is your reason for coming here?"

I thought for a moment. Obviously, he is looking for something specific here. Leaning forward I set down my cup on one of the unmatched coasters lying on the table. "Well, I suppose I am here because the board of directors told me to come. So, I feel like I need to be here…to get… what?"

"Go on," the old man waved his hand at me to continue.

"Because I'm up for this promotion, a big one, and they said it is part of the vetting process."

"Ah, yes." The man nodded. "And you want this job? This promotion?"

"Yes, I do. It would mean a great deal to me. I've worked hard to get where I am."

"Indeed."

He sat for another several minutes without speaking, sipping the tea and gazing out the window at the park. I glanced around the room, hoping to land upon a clock, but I could not find one anywhere in the apartment.

We sat this way longer than I could calculate. He did not speak, but every now and then sipped at his tea. I finished mine out of politeness, waiting for him to speak and unable to comprehend what was happening.

"Okay," he said after carefully setting down his cup. "We are finished."

I stood up and watched him rise from his chair, a slow and arduous process involving a lot of careful balance. He crossed the room and walked towards the desk tucked in the corner of the room. I thought that perhaps he would give me the note I needed to give Benjamin, the clearance he needed, but it was not to be. He picked up a pen and marked a figure on the desktop calendar.

"You will come back again next week. Same time."

"Next week!" I exclaimed, unable to hide my disappointment.

He said, "Yes next week, because you'll choose to."

"Look, I need you to give your approval or whatever this is about, so I can get this promotion and get on with my life."

As soon as the words escaped me, I realized how rude they had sounded, but it was too late. He stood up straight and walked over to me, in that same careful movement he had done everything in. With his wrinkled hand, he reached up and patted me on the cheek. He gazed into my face, with a twinkle in his eye and expression of one examining a gift horse.

"Next week," he said. He turned and walked to the chair, sitting down once more and returning his gaze out the window.

Without another word, I saw myself out.

***

"How did it go?" Nikki asked when I arrived home that evening.

"To tell the truth, I'm not sure. He didn't really do much." I must have sounded as confused as I felt.

"So what did he do?" She put down her crossword and looked up at me, genuine curiosity on her face.

I explained the bizarre events as they happened, including the long expanse of time when he simply sat without speaking. As I finished the tale, she smiled, before breaking into laughter.

"What's so funny?" I asked.

"You could stand to slow down every now and then, you know."

"What is that supposed to mean?"

"I mean, you get so caught up in getting things done, that you don't take a minute to enjoy what's around you."

"I enjoy what's around me," I insisted.

"Oh, really? What did we have for dinner?"

"That's just silly. I know what we had for dinner."

"Okay, what was it?" She broke out in a playful grin waiting for my answer.

The truth was, she had caught me. Of course, I had been at the table, but I was so focused on the messages between myself, Dave and another teammate, that I inhaled the food, taking bites between punching out replies. I barely remembered.

"Chicken?" I guessed.

She threw the embroidered pillow at me. "Pork chops!"

"That was what I meant!" I ducked and she laughed

with that iridescent sound that made me fall in love with her in the first place, all those years ago.

"Dad," my son says from the hallway. "Are you coming to the game next month."

"Is it baseball season already?" I asked, incredulously.

"Yes," Nikki chided. "We told you about it at dinner, remember?"

"Of course. Let me add it to my schedule." He watched, peering over my shoulder as I punch the details into the calendar in my phone. "There. I'll be there or else."

***

I had almost forgotten about the bizarre meeting with the park vendor when Frank Benjamin popped his head into my office. "Still got those financial reports coming?" he asked.

"Yes, I'm just sending out the email right now."

"Good man." He nearly disappeared.

"Mr. Benjamin," I called out and he looked back into the office.

"Yes?"

"I wanted to talk to you about the man I met in the park yesterday. I think there has to be some kind of mistake."

"Oh? What mistake is that?"

"He's not at all what I thought he would be."

"How so?"

"He's a park vendor. He's not a business guru. I don't get it."

"I didn't want to tell you this, but it's not really about you, Kumar."

"I don't understand."

"You know how sometimes there's a program where the foster kids come and read library books to the dogs in the shelters?"

I didn't, but I motioned for him to continue.

"Do you think any of the dogs care one bit about having stories read to them?"

"Probably not."

"Think of it like that. I think this guy is the uncle of one of the board members or something. He just needs someone to look in on him every now and then. Makes him feel like he has something to do."

"I see," I replied. "But what has that got to do with the promotion?"

"Red tape, my boy. Red tape. Sometimes you just have to play the game."

"Wait, so am I the dog or the foster kid in this scenario?"

He shrugged before he vanished once more. I felt even more confused than ever. I turned my attention back to the emails and reports.

Chapter Five

*"Never let the odds keep you from pursuing what you
know in your heart you were meant to do."*
– Satchel Paige

I had planned on getting out of it, one way or another;
but one week later, I found myself standing in front of the
apartment door of the park vendor. I couldn't decide how
or why I had arrived there. With some trepidation, I tapped
on the door.

"I'm doing this as a service" I told myself. "This isn't
about me."

But in the back of my mind, I kept thinking about that
promotion.

"Hello, come in!" he said with a smile. "Look what I
have found."

I stepped inside and watched him bustle back to the
center of the room. A large, woven basket sat on the coffee
table. He delighted and fussed over the blankets around the
edges. In the center of the basket I spotted a rolling pile of
tawny fur, which took me a moment to recognize as kittens.
There were four in all, three orange tabbies and one gray
one with blue eyes. I could not help but be momentarily
taken by them. He picked one up, the kitten's wide eyes
gazing about the room, and letting out a 'meow', which
sounded like an accusation.

"Here," he said, placing the kitten in my hand.

"Oh, I don't—" But it was already settling into my
grasp. I held up the tiny creature and peered plaintively into

its face. The kitten blinked. "Where did you find them?" I asked.

"At my doorstep this morning. Aren't they lovely?"

"They're cute." I couldn't deny it. They were. "What will you do with them?"

"Do? Why, I'll take care of them of course, until such time as I cannot."

I wondered at the old man, his bony fingers gently caressing each kitten as it squirmed in the towel lined basket. His face lit up like a child on Christmas morning. He motioned for me to sit, and I watched him pour out a few saucers of milk and set them down on the table, placing each kitten next to a bowl.

"So," he said. "Tell me about your week."

"It has been fine. Nothing to speak of really."

"That can't be right," he replied, continuing to watch the kittens explore the apartment and sniff around the legs of the table.

It wasn't. I didn't want to talk about it, honestly. I had a fight with Nikki a few days prior and the stain of it still hung over our household, despite our best efforts of keeping it from the kids.

"Well, work is fine," I said.

"But?"

It occurred to me that the only people I had in my life in any capacity were Dave and Frank Benjamin. Sure, there were co-workers, but no real friendships besides Nikki and she was angry with me.

"Something is troubling you. I can see it in your countenance You will always have a challenge."

"That's obvious?"

"No, that's life," he answered simply, nodding with a

bemused expression as one of the kittens trotted across my lap, it's swishing tail hitting me in the face. I grimaced and waved away the puff of shedding fur left by the action.

"My wife," I began. "She wants me to reconsider this promotion I've been offered. She says I already spend too much time away from home."

"Does it not make you happy?" he asked. "That she would want you to do this?"

"I just don't get it," I replied, waving my hands in front of me. "I mean, the whole reason I've worked so hard is to make things better for my family. I did what I had to do to get a good job and with this promotion it will make it so she doesn't have to work anymore."

"What does she do now?"

"She works part time at a dress shop while the kids are in school. I even told her she didn't have to do that, but she said she needed to get out of the house."

Shah sat and watched me. I could tell there was something going on behind his eyes. He squinted and set his gaze level upon me.

"What?" I asked.

One of the kittens had crawled up the side of the couch, found its way down the top edge and stuck its wet nose into my ear. I jumped and brushed the kitten away. Shah laughed at my reaction, clapping his hands together as the kitten found his footing, scurrying down and across the floor, disappearing behind Shah's feet.

I suppressed a surge of annoyance. "What do you think I should do?"

"About the kitten?" Shah smiled at me.

"About my wife."

"Ah." He settled back in his chair, letting one of the

small creatures curl up in the bowl of his lap. "Well, what is the problem with your wife wishing you to spend time with your family?"

"I just...I'm doing the best I can already."

"Is that so?"

"I make enough money to support the family," I explained. "But getting this promotion would really turn things around for us. I could possibly plan towards an early retirement. This should make things easier for her. She can quit her job if she wants to. I don't know, I just don't get it."

"Was it necessary for your wife to take the job at the dress shop?"

Shrugging I answered, "Not really."

"So why did she take it then?"

"She said she needed out of the house." I paused for a moment and looked Shah in the eye. "Wait, what are you getting at? Do you think she's just bored?"

Before he answered, the little gray kitten stretched against my leg. The tiny claws pierced through my pants and pricked against my skin, once more interrupting my train of thought. Shah laughed at the antics.

"Can we put these cats in the bathroom, or something until we finish?" I snapped. "I can't even concentrate on what I want to say."

Shah stood, crossed the room and bent down towards the small kitten. With surprising agility he scooped it up, placing it back in the basket. The kitten hopped over with a playful 'meow', leaping after Shah's sleeve trailing down from his bony arm.

"You're not seeing the order from your perceived chaos," Shah said. "It is an impossible task."

"I don't understand what you mean?"

"Do you want her to be fulfilled?"

"My wife? Of course I do, but she should be happy. I'm doing this for her and the kids. I don't understand why she doesn't see that." A flush of heat began to rise in my cheeks.

"Are you?"

"Of course I am!" I stood and stalked across the room, pacing back and forth in the small apartment.

"Hm," he gently stroked the kitten on his lap, while his other hand scratched behind the ears of one perched on the arm of his chair. "These kittens, how do you think they came to be here?"

"You said someone left them at your doorstep."

"But why here?" he continued. "Why not out there in the middle of the parking lot?"

"That's ridiculous. They could get hit by a car."

"Or someone could have found them there as well. Why do you think someone took the extra step towards placing them close to a door?"

"So you would find them and take care of them."

Shah looked at me with excitement and exclaimed, "Do you see?"

"Not really." I had calmed down a bit and I returned to my place on the couch. "What does that have to do with anything?"

"Perhaps nothing." The pale orange kitten next to him hopped down to the floor. "Often people will seek happiness rather than fulfillment."

"What's the difference?" I questioned, running my fingers through my hair.

"What makes you fulfilled, Kumar? Do not answer right away. I would like for you to think about it."

I sighed, unable to mask my annoyance. "Okay, fine. I'll play along. I enjoy my job."

"And that makes you joyous?" He pointed a knobby finger towards me. "There is a difference. Think harder."

What makes me fulfilled, I wondered? I thought back to the last time I felt like I had experienced true joy, those moments here and there which were indicators of happiness in the purest form. The taste of the finest wine, the adrenaline of leaping off a bungee platform, the heady rush of seeing Nikki smile. When was the last time I had felt anything like that?

"Well, I guess you could say that it makes me happy to be able to take care of the people I love."

"You do not seem happy right now."

"Because what I do is not being appreciated!"

"Happiness is a result of doing, but fulfillment is the ability to see order from disorder. Happiness is a lost cause. We all want to be loved and appreciated for who we really are."

"Well, that's encouraging," I muttered.

He nodded.

After a few minutes of silence followed by our "goodbyes", I left. I felt weirdly put off by the conversation, still rolling over the scenario in my mind. I decided to head back to work and take the afternoon to finish up the spreadsheets for the week.

***

"The proof is in the pudding!" Frank Benjamin bellowed from his seat behind his large oak desk. "You have consistently produced the wanted results and are therefore the most qualified for this position."

"Sir," I said, sitting across from him. "I wanted to talk to you about that."

"What's to talk about? This is a dream opportunity for anyone."

I folded my fingers together, thinking about how I wanted to word what I wanted to say. "Mr. Benjamin," I began. "I want to discuss something with you. Purely hypothetical, of course."

"Of course, my boy. My door is always open. You know that."

"Mr. Benjamin, I want to ask, what would happen with the company if I decided to decline the promotion."

"Decline the promotion?" His voice boomed through the spacious office. "I won't hear of it!"

"Bear with me sir," I said, raising my hands. "There are some concerns I'd at least like to talk about."

He paused then, leaning forward and placing his elbows on his desk. He drew his eyebrows together and took me in with his steady gaze. "What is it? What's troubling you?"

"I don't know if anything is troubling me exactly, but I would like to know what significant changes would happen once I accept the position."

"You would have a higher percentage going into your 401K for one. A larger percentage of stocks. That's money in your pocket."

"I guess so."

"Actually, I'm glad you came by. There is a luncheon next week which I'd like you to attend with me. It was meant to be a surprise but you've been nominated as one of the Five Under Fifty. It's a pretty high honor."

"That is an honor," I replied, taken aback. "I don't know what to say."

"Say you'll be there!" His mouth stretched into a grin.

I felt speechless at the offer. The Five Under Fifty award was sought after by every corporate business person in the city. And it would put my face on Forbes magazine. They liked to run a whole issue featuring each of the nominees. For a moment, I was flabbergasted that I would even be considered.

"Well? You'll be there, right?"

"Of course, sir. It's an honor. Thank you."

"I didn't nominate you, but I do heartily agree with whoever did. Now something was bothering you. Do you care to tell me about that?"

"It's nothing, truly. I appreciate your concern. I'm just trying to make sure all my bases are covered. You understand that, sir?"

"Of course. That's why you get the results you do, my boy. You are thorough. Nothing wrong with that."

"Thank you, sir." I brushed my hands across my thighs as I stood ready to leave.

"I'll have Cynthia send the email with the information about the award luncheon and the magazine spread."

"I'll keep an eye out. Thank you, sir."

"Oh, and Kumar…"

"Yes?" I turned back to face him at the door.

"I'm excited to see what kind of results you'll get once you have the company at your disposal. These are exciting times."

"Yes, sir. Thank you," I walked out of his office with a spring in my step, closing the door behind me and waving at Cynthia, who returned a cheerful smile.

I ran into Dave halfway down the hallway to my office.

"Hey there, Big Shot," he said, patting me on the back.

"You up for a round of golf later?"

"Yeah, that sounds good. I'll catch up with you." A 9 holes would be good for me to clear my head, I decided. The rest of the day was spent in a hazy headache as I completed the spreadsheets for the week. The conversation with Benjamin had done little to ease my mind and I felt at odds with myself for reasons I could not pin point.

At 4:45 I picked up my gym bag, locked the office door behind me, and headed down the hall to grab Dave before heading out to the park.

Chapter Six

*"Define success on your own terms, achieve it by your
own rules, and build a life you're proud to live."*
−Anne Sweeney

"So what does he do?" Dave asked after tossing the
disc towards the far-off basket.

"I'm not sure exactly," I replied taking my place at the
tee platform. "Benjamin wanted me to go see him. The
board of directors wanted me to do it. Some kind of service
deal for my promotion. I think they want me to remember
the little people or something along those lines."

"So you just talk to him?"

"Sort of like that. He talks to me mostly. Asks me
questions about my day."

"What kind of stuff does he talk about?"

"Just different things. This time, he had a basket of
kittens someone had left at his front door."

Dave laughed as we parted ways, each walking towards
where our discs had landed. I took aim towards the basket.
Maybe, this time, I would make par. The disc flew from
my fingertips, arcing through the air towards its mark. I
strolled towards Dave who also took aim.

"How long do you have to go see him?"

"I'm not sure. There is supposed to be some sign off or
something so I can get the promotion."

"Ah, the promotion."

I paused and looked Dave in the eye. "Hey, I don't
want it to be weird. I know you wanted it too."

"It won't be weird. Why would it be weird? I'm doing okay." He picked up his disc and tossed it the last few feet into the basket.

"You got par on this one. Good job."

"I'm par for the course, right now," Dave grinned as we collected our discs, heading towards the next tee.

"I don't think I'm going to see him anymore," I said.

"Why not? What about your promotion?"

"I should get it either way. I mean what should it matter if I go and talk to an elderly park vendor once a week? I think I have more than proven myself for this. Don't you?"

Dave stopped walking and stared at me with his mouth open. "Wow," he muttered.

"What?" I stopped and hitched my disc bag up on my shoulder.

"Would you listen to yourself right now?"

"What?" I take my place at the front of the next tee, pausing to consider which direction to take aim. "What are you talking about?" I let go of the disc.

"You are starting to sound like an arrogant blowhard, Kumar."

His words stung, but only a little bit. "Do you think so?"

"Yeah, I think so. You are on the brink of having everything you've ever wanted in life, yet you can't take an hour out of your week to spend some time with a lonely old man." He shook his head. "Wow."

"It's not like that, Dave. Honest. You should meet him. To you and me he seems just like a park vendor. I don't even know what he does there. Kebobs or something, and he always has sports drinks for the joggers; hands out samples for the kids. It's quite remarkable."

"Yeah?" Dave stepped up to the tee, stepping into the throw. The disc flew wildly into the air, wobbling. I felt sure it would fall, but just at the arc the wind caught it and it sailed the rest of the way towards the basket at the other end of the field.

"Lucky break there," I said nodding towards his disc, now lying closer to the basket than my own.

"So you think," he replied with a smirk.

We walked along, the silence growing between us. My mind reeled and once more I could not pin-point the reason why.

"Can I ask you a question?" I said as we crested the slope in the field.

"Sure, man," Dave replied, affably.

"How do you define success?"

He paused to pick up his disk, twirling it between his palms as he considered. "I think it means different things to different people. Why do you ask that question?"

I shrugged. "I guess I always thought of it as one thing, you know? The car, the house, the dinners. To me that's what success looks like; has always looked like."

"But…" he motioned for me to continue.

"But now that I'm here, it just doesn't feel right."

"What does it feel like?"

"I can't say really." I tossed my disc into the basket, causing a faint clink as the chains rattle together. "How do you mean?"

"Mean what?"

"That it means different things to different people?"

"You know," he paused as he looked up at the sky. "When I was first working for the company, before I got hired into the corporate side, I worked IT for the call center.

They used to have these theme days to try and boost morale or whatever. So they would have team days where the staff could wear their favorite sports tee shirt, stuff like that."

"Right," I nodded.

"But there was this one girl who always fought it. She always said she didn't want to participate, and most of the time they didn't make her. But one day the theme for the day was 'Dress for Success'. Everyone was told to dress up in their best business attire for the one day. No one ever pointed it out, but these days always fell on the same days the corporate clients would come visit. Make it look good, you know."

I snorted in laughter. "That's pretty sneaky."

"So this one girl, I heard her ask, what did they mean by success? What if, she said, someone wanted to be a successful chef. Can they wear a chef's uniform? Or a successful astronaut or scuba diver?"

"What did they tell her?"

"They told her she was being difficult and to stop causing problems."

"Of course." We picked up our discs and moved on.

"But I guess," he continued. "I guess that has always stuck with me on some level. Because she's right. Here the management was trying to impress this one version of success on these people, but the truth is it can mean whatever you decide it means. I just don't think people allow themselves the permission to be aligned with their success."

I considered his words for a moment.

He continued, "Take me for example. We were both in consideration for the VP slot, right?"

"Yeah," I shuffled my feet trying to dispel the perceived

awkwardness surrounding the topic. "About that…"

"No, hang on," Dave insisted, holding up his hand. "Hear me out. I don't think we are seeing this the same way. I'm perfectly fine that the board chose you over me."

"Really?" I turned to face him and his countenance appeared to hold with the sincerity of his words.

"Really, Kumar. I'm happy for you. I came into this career path wanting long term security. I have that. Now I am able to be with my family when they need me. I've succeeded in what I want."

"But don't you ever want more than that?"

"More? Yes, but more of what I want, not what others think I want. Do you, Kumar?" He tossed the disc.

I did not answer but for the remainder of the back nine, I rolled his words over in my head. The conversation shifted then to more skin-deep topics, like kids in school and how our teams were doing in sports.

* * *

"You're just in time," Nikki said as I walked in the front door. The scent of roasted something and stir-fried vegetables encountered my senses, making my mouth water.

"I went to the park with Dave."

"It'd be nice if you could spend some of that spare time with me, you know." Her words held a tinge of seriousness but she spoke with a smile, twisting around to look at me from the stove. Both kids sat at the table doing their homework.

"Hi, Dad!"

"Hi guys, how was school?"

"Fine," replied my daughter with a wrinkle in her nose. "Go shower, Dad. You smell like sweat!"

"I'll be right back." I paused at the stove to kiss Nikki on her lovely, olive neck.

"Go on!" she shrieked. "You do smell like sweat." She shooed me away with a toss of the kitchen towel. I gave her a smile, flicking the towel back before exiting the kitchen.

Chapter Seven

*"When I was a boy of fourteen, my father was so ignorant
I could hardly stand to have the old man around. But
when I got to be twenty-one, I was astonished at how
much the old man had learned in seven years."*
—Mark Twain

"Where did they go?" I asked, looking for the kittens, as I stepped into Shah's apartment.

"I have found homes for all of them," Shah said, stepping back to allow me inside the small apartment. The sun shone through the window, creating a golden square upon his shabby carpet. He motioned for me to have a seat on the couch.

"All of them?" I replied. "That's impressive."

"Not so much." He waved his hand, dismissing my remark. "All I had to do was bring them with me one day to the park. The people came and the kittens went. They were all with new families by noon."

He puttered around his kitchen corner once more, finally settling on his chair like a bee on a flower. I continued to be amazed at his agility. If I had to guess, he had to be at least seventy. He offered me tea but I declined this time.

"They are such funny little creatures," he said.

"What, the cats?"

"Yes. Having them around is such a great reminder of the important things."

"How do you mean?" I asked, as I could hardly fathom how those pesky little creatures could reveal the secrets of the universe.

He chuckled before pointing one of his gnarled fingers in my direction. "Animals are creatures of instinct."

"And people are not?" I questioned, finding myself curious about his line of thought. I had learned that he could go on a tangent at any moment.

"People could be as well, but most often they suppress their instincts, opting instead for what they should do."

"I don't understand." I leaned back, propping my foot up on my knee and clasping my hands around my knee, waiting for his response.

"What makes a successful businessman?" Shah asked.

"That's easy," I said. "Money."

He laughed a dry cackle, which caught his breath long enough that I wondered if I should go and pat his back. "No," he gasped at last. "No. The answer is instinct."

"How do you figure?"

"Think about the kittens for a moment."

"Okay." *This should be interesting.*

"While they were here, you asked me to put them in the bathroom until the end of our talk."

"Yes, I remember that."

"Yet, if I had done that, would they have ceased being kittens?"

"What?"

"Just answer." He nodded, with a knowing grin.

"No, they would not have ceased being kittens."

"And as such, they would have played and frolicked and probably torn up the bathroom, wouldn't you say?"

"Most likely," I replied. I had no idea where he was going with this.

"So your desire was to remove them from being an inconvenience for you, but I would still have had to experience the consequences of putting them away. Either the challenge of having them with us, running around and playing, or the challenge *later* of having all the paper shredded in the bathroom. Do you see?"

"I guess so, but what does that have to do with instinct?"

"If you put an animal in a cage, it is still that animal. A cat will still play. A lion will still roar. The essence of the animal will remain intact. Then, one day it will burst forth. It cannot be suppressed. It is the same with a man."

"How so?"

"People are meant to live by instinct, not by logic."

"But logic is what separates us from the animals," I questioned puzzled at his hypothesis. "Is it not?"

"One would think, but perhaps it is contrary, it is the alignment of logic and instinct."

"Can I ask you a question?" I said, suddenly wishing to change the subject.

"Of course."

"How did you become a park vendor?"

He tented his fingertips together and pressed them to his chin, drawing in his eyebrows. "The answer may surprise you."

"I'd like to hear. We talk so much about me and philosophies. I'd like to hear your story."

"Alright," he settled in and gazed up at the ceiling. "I decided I wanted to be of service to those around me." With that, he fell silent. I waited for him to continue, but he simply tapped his fingertips together in a row.

"That's it?" I asked, prodding for more.

"What more is there?" he said. "Being of service to others is the greatest thing a man can do."

"But just a moment ago, you said that putting an animal

in a cage suppresses their instinct. How is being beholden to others any different? Isn't that the same as being in a cage?"

"I was already in a cage of my own doing," he said. "A cage from which I never thought I could escape. Walking away from it, choosing this life, has made me free. More than I have ever been."

"Because you came to America?"

"I chose to come to America because it was the best place for me to be."

I shook my head trying to make sense of his random and vague answers. He had answered me, but I still felt as if I knew nothing about him. Nothing more than I had a moment ago.

"You must focus on the service first and then the results will follow."

"What the heck is that supposed to mean?" I said.

"You should try it," he said snapping his gaze to me all of a sudden. "Tell me, Kumar. When you were a boy, what did you say you wanted to be?"

"Well, my father was a doctor and I guess it was always assumed that I would be too."

"Hm…" he tapped his fingers again, clearly dissatisfied with my answer.

"Fine!" I threw my hands up in the air. "That's not what you are asking, is it?"

With an infuriating calmness, he shook his head. "No. It is not."

"What I wanted to be?" I rolled my eyes away from him and thought for a moment. "Horses," I replied at last. "I always wanted to work with horses."

He did not answer right away, but watched me as the

memory played across my mind, perhaps revealing itself in my expression. He continued to listen, unmoving but with a distant and appreciative smile on his face.

"I haven't thought about it for years," I continued. "But I must have been about seven years old the first time I saw them. My parents had taken me to a ranch for kids as a reward for making good grades. That was something that didn't happen often, so when it did, they kind of made a big deal out of it. But I remember seeing them running in the field even before we had made it to the gate. They were so beautiful. More majestic than anything I had ever seen before."

Shah simply looked at me and smiled, as I relived my memory of the ranch. Snapping out of it, I glanced at my watch and realized it was time to leave if I wanted to get home before Nikki and the kids had eaten dinner. Saying goodbye, I left Shah's with a sense of calm, remembering the galloping horses from my memory.

***

The luncheon was laid out against the back wall. Dishes and platters were stacked on a table draped in white linen. Against each end of the table stood the banquet servers in their black pants and starched white shirts, hands clasped behind their backs waiting for the cue to begin service. Each round table held six seats and opulent centerpieces, globed candles and gold edged plates.

"Not a bad set up, eh?" my boss said, nudging me.

"No sir," I replied. "Not bad at all."

"This is just the beginning," he said. "I see big things in your future."

"Thank you, sir."

We took our places at the table marked with a white card in the middle of the display, emblazoned with the name of our corporation. Each subsequent table had the names of the appropriate company on it as well. All around us, the people streamed in, chatting and taking sips of the ice water already placed at the table. The room contained a magnificence with which I was unfamiliar.

"This is part of what I wanted to talk to you about, Kumar."

"What is that?"

"Today they will be making the announcement of the nominees. We'll have to arrange for your spread in Forbes magazine. You know you'll need to prepare for an interview."

"I assumed as much. I've already started to take some notes for it."

"I want you to think about some of the points, like being results driven as we talked about the other day." He dropped his voice as someone took the stage welcoming us all to the event. Benjamin leaned in and completed his thoughts, "I think you should include some other points as well. We'll discuss it more afterward."

The nominating event went forward with all the pomp and ceremony that goes along with it. After the welcoming, the banquet servers sprang into action, streaming out of the side doors with trays ladened with silver topped plates. With machine-like precision, they placed the trays on the tables and picked up the plates three at a time, circling us and placing the dishes before us. As if on cue each silver dome was lifted up to reveal our entree. Baskets of steaming bread replaced the centerpieces. Wine was poured and just like that everyone had been served.

The director of the event took the stage after everyone had a chance to begin their meal. Once more we were welcomed and told that the nominees were about to be named.

"I hope you don't mind," Benjamin said leaning over to me, "I had to write a bio for you. Hope it does you justice."

Before each name was given, the director gave a list of accomplishments for the Five Under Fifty nominees. One was a tech genius who made his fortune in Silicon Valley and later returned to the Chicago area, starting a business that promoted the tech industry and created opportunities for school children in poverty-stricken areas of the city. Another was the first woman to break the billion dollar mark with her start-up, which stemmed from philanthropy and charity work within the city.

"Our next nominee," the speaker continued, "can be recognized as one of the first young men to reach the position of Vice President within his first five years at the company. Named for his remarkable sales turnover, this nominee is known for being results driven with an almost animalistic ferocity."

Benjamin reached over and chucked me on the shoulder. His expression was one of pride, though I could not determine if it was towards me or towards the wording of the bio, which he had submitted and was currently being read.

"I am proud to name our next nominee for the Five Under Fifty Award—Kumar Vedig!"

The applause followed, polite and appropriate, as I stood and waved to the gathered corporates, just as the other nominees had done. I felt wildly out of place as I sat down and the speaker continued with the remaining names. I listened closely to each bio and instantly realized that mine was the only one missing a service aspect. Urban outreach, mentorship, even animal rights were mentioned for one nominee. Although the day was to celebrate me and the others, and Frank Benjamin was beaming at me from his seat as the applause rose around us, I felt hollow inside.

Results, success, ferocity.

I thought about what Shah had said about putting an animal in a cage. Was I in that cage, I wondered?

"What do you say we get out of here and go get ourselves some steaks?" Benjamin asked as the event came to an end.

"But we have just had lunch," I pointed out.

"This barely put a drop in the bucket," he replied patting his sizeable stomach. "Do you think I got this good looking by sticking with salad and upper crust fair?" He nudged my elbow. "Besides, there is more I want to talk to you about."

We exited and he motioned for me to come with him. He had his own driver. I already knew this, but had never been privy to the experience before. True to his word, we circled the corner and stopped at a local steakhouse.

"This is more my kind of scene," he said with a hefty chortle. "How do you like yours?"

"Uh, medium rare, I guess,"

"That's my boy!" He patted me once more on the shoulder as we approached the front door of the restaurant.

We settled into plush seats at the rough-hewn oaken table, which went well with the rest of the surrounding décor of deer heads and shotguns. A server walked by with steaming plates of loaded baked potatoes and huge slabs of beef.

"How many times have you had lunch twice, my boy?" Benjamin asked.

"I would have to say this is probably the first," I replied.

"Well, it won't be the last." He turns to the server. "Two of your steak specials. Medium rare, leaning to rare—if you know what I mean—and a couple of ice teas."

The server jotted down the order and whisked away to gather our drinks.

"I'm glad we are able to sit down for a minute, Kumar," Benjamin began. I could tell by his posture that he was gearing up to leap into a diatribe. "Once we move through the paperwork to move you into the VP slot, you'll have some changes, big changes coming. I'd like to ask you, how do you think you might fit within those changes?"

"I'm not sure I understand what you mean, sir," I said, at a loss of what he was asking me.

"I mean, where do you *fit* in a perfect world? What do you *see* yourself doing with this opportunity?"

I considered his words. In a way, they echoed the question that Shah had asked me a few days earlier.

"Well, of course, I want to take part in the decision-making processes which impact the company. I'd like to find a way to create growth in the production segment of our industry."

Benjamin shook his head as if reacting to an errant child. "Kumar, you sound like you are giving me what you think I want to hear. I have no doubt you will be elemental in the betterment of this company. What I'm asking is, what do you want? What makes Kumar tick?"

I rolled over the answer I had given Shah. Benjamin sat across from me, his elbows leaned just at the edge of the table, his torso tilted forward. His eyes gleamed with a genuine desire to hear my answer. In the briefest moment, I saw—for once—not the man who was my boss, but

Frank Benjamin, just another man caught in the machine of corporate America. A man like me, waiting to hear my answer.

"I've always wanted to work with horses," I blurted out the information before I had a chance to consider. "When I was a kid, there was this day camp I got to attend one weekend. I thought they were the most incredible creatures..." My explanation petered out when I saw his expression change from interest to puzzlement.

"Horses, eh?" he said, shifting in his chair.

"It was just a childhood fancy," I said. "Nothing I ever took any action on."

"Good thing too, right? I mean look at you *now*."

Our steaks arrived, and upon seeing the glistening slab of meat set before me, I had to admit that the modern presentation of the meal from the nomination luncheon had merely whetted my appetite. I joined in with Benjamin, diving into the meal with appropriate gusto, enjoying every bite.

"You've got a good instinct, Kumar," he said between bites. "I don't want you to lose that. I doubt that you will, but hold on to it. Could be that one day you'll be running this company."

"I don't aspire to that, sir."

"No?" His eyebrows shot halfway up his forehead. "You should! How do you think I got here? You remind me quite a bit of myself, Kumar. When I was your age, I would never have dreamed of running this company. I have to retire someday, and you've done an excellent job of positioning yourself for success. I had nothing to do with that."

"Maybe not." Though I could not help but wonder how

much of Benjamin's mentorship had an effect on what I was doing with my life. Not that I didn't appreciate it. I did, greatly. The protein buzz from the steak combined with the wine from lunch made for a heady combination.

We finished the day with a round of drinks at the bar. One thing I noticed about Frank Benjamin is that he does nothing halfway. Perhaps that attributed somewhat to his success. I told myself to make a note to pick up his book, which he published a few years ago. *The Money Secrets of Frank Benjamin*. Not that I'd have anything to worry about in that regard either. Being VP of the company would set me and my family up for life. The opportunity was more than I could hope for.

Dinner had long past by the time I finally arrived home. The kids had gone to bed and my wife sat in the living room tapping out something on her computer, a tablet with an attached keyboard, perched on her knees.

"Sorry, I'm home late," I said, placing my briefcase on the couch and loosening my tie. I knew she would understand it eventually.

"You missed the baseball game," she replied without looking up.

"Oh, Nikki. Dammit. Was that tonight? I'm so sorry. I was with the boss. I couldn't get away."

She closed her tablet, crossing her hands over the top of it. "I'm not the one you need to apologize to, Kumar." With that, she stood and disappeared down the hallway.

Chapter Eight

"The road to success and the road to failure are almost exactly the same."

–Colin R. Davis

I showed up at my office to find all of my desk items in a box on my office chair. At first, I experience a wave of dizziness. Had something gone wrong?

"Hey, big man!" Dave shouted as he approached from his office down the hallway. "Have you heard?"

"Heard what? What's going on?"

"You've been reassigned."

There was still a small part of me thinking I had been fired due to some unforeseen event. Maybe the board member thought I was rude to his grandfather or something. I turned and saw Benjamin approaching from the other end of the hallway. His face was twisted with intensity.

"Kumar," he called. "Moving day!"

I stood still, waiting to hear the outcome. My hands felt like they were made of lead. Benjamin sidled up next to me, placing one thick arm around my shoulders.

"You ready to see your new office?"

I could not suppress the smile erupting across my face. "Let's go," I said, feeling a surge of pride and accomplishment. Benjamin dragged me down the hall with Dave following behind us.

The view from the floor to ceiling windows was that of the skyline—pristine and sparkling in the morning sunlight. The glistening reflection of the Chicago River wound through the city, blinding sunlight and reflecting the clear surge of happiness plastered on my face.

Benjamin motioned for me to step inside the office. The desk was an onyx slab, modern and streamlined. Bookshelves lined the inner wall where I could finally display the tombs of company history piled in the corner in my old office. Dave stepped forward and handed me the box he brought from my old office. I took it and set it on the corner of the desk.

"I don't know what to say." I turned and faced the two of them, taking in the expansive space.

"You've done it, son," Benjamin boomed. "You have arrived."

"So it would seem."

Behind him some of the other employees appeared, filtering through the door. Cynthia carried a large platter bearing a white frosted cake with the words, "Congrats!" imprinted across the top. She set it down on the desk and pulled out a knife, slicing into the creamy, white frosting to reveal the moist devil's food cake hidden underneath. The party lasted into the afternoon. One by one over the course of the day, everyone approached me to offer their congratulations.

Cynthia walked up to me, her glasses perched at the end of her powdered nose. "Oh, look," she said. "You've got a bit of frosting." She reached up and wiped my face with the pad of her thumb, a maternal gesture. "There, that's got it."

I glanced at her, leaning against the edge of the desk next to me.

"Tell me something, Cynthia," I said.

"Yes, Kumar?" She sipped at a plastic cup of lemon soda.

"How long have you been with the company?"

"Oh, quite a while," she simpered. "I started when I was twenty-five. I was young."

"Have you been a receptionist the whole time?"

She paused, tapping her fingertips against her chin. "I never really thought about it; but yes, I believe I have."

"Did you ever consider getting into the business end? You have a wonderful personality. A real skill at making people feel like they are being taken care of."

She smiled and waved her hand. "Oh, I don't know about that."

"No, I'm serious. I mean, I know you have seniority over many of these new, young sales people. You've probably seen more than a few of them put together. I'm sure you could show them a thing or two."

She laughed and shook her head. "I never considered it, to be honest."

"Are you happy in your job here?"

"Do I have anything to worry about?" she asked placing her hand at her fine gold necklace.

"Oh, no! Not at all. That's not what I meant!"

She laughed again, her eyes sparkled. "I know, but to answer your question, yes. I am happy in this job. I've never wanted for anything, and I've had security in my life. That's something not everyone can say."

"I guess you're right," I replied.

She raised her cup in an impromptu cheer before walking away towards some of the other employees clustered at the other end of the office. I caught Benjamin watching me with a proud glance. Dave interrupted my thoughts, approaching with a slab of cake balanced on his tiny plate.

"Hey, you want to hit the park after all this? Work off the cake?"

"You're one to talk. What is that, your third slice?"

He chuckled. "What can I say, when plenty arrives, one must take advantage of it."

"You almost sound like Shah," I said with a laugh.

"How is all that going?" he asked.

"It's weird. I thought that after I got this promotion I wouldn't have to see him anymore, but as it stands, I don't know if I should stop. I'm finding that I want to go and tell him about it."

"Hm.," Dave replied.

"What?"

"Nothing, nothing at all." He wandered off, licking the icing off his fork.

***

The fresh air felt good after the office filled with fellow employees, no matter how big the room might have been. Benjamin had pushed for us to go out for celebratory drinks, and the thought was tempting. In the end, Dave saved us with a cheap shot about our wives being at home waiting for us.

"The old ball and chain, you know," he had said. Benjamin had nodded wisely and dismissed us with a wave of his hand.

***

"I have something for you!" Shah exclaimed as he waved me into the apartment. He hobbled over to the table next to his chair, flipping through a small pile of envelopes. I stepped inside and perched on the edge of the couch, waiting. "Here," he said, handing me a brochure with a slip of paper tucked into the middle fold. "Have a look."

I glanced down, flipping through with some confusion. The front flap showed a collage of smiling faces; a young Asian child on a horse, a dark-haired woman smiling up at the child and clutching the horse's lead. The background appeared to be a distant range of foothills and pastures. Sunshine Equine Camp was printed in cheerful yellow font across the top.

"What is this?" I asked, looking up at Shah in confusion.

"It is what you wanted. Your horses from when you were a boy. You can volunteer. I found it for you!" His expression seemed almost comical, the way he kept gesturing towards the pamphlet in my hand, his mouth stretched back, revealing his bare gums, eyes gleaming.

"I don't understand," I said, a statement which had become more frequent during my chats with Shah.

"What's not to understand? You told me you have always wanted to do it, so go and do it."

I considered his words and upon examining his lifestyle, it became apparent to me some time ago that he did not have access to the internet or a means of transportation outside of city transit. However he had done it, it must have taken him some effort to track down this brochure for me. I had to tread carefully on how I should respond.

"I can't," I replied.

"You can't or you won't."

"Shah, I just have too much going on right now. This job coming up and all the changes which come along with that. It's just not feasible."

"This job that you do, what does it entail?"

"Any number of things," I replied. "Financial spreadsheets, performance reviews, predictions for yearly quota, that sort of stuff."

"Sounds fascinating. Does this work, these spreadsheets and predictions, do they bring you joy?"

"Well, sure. I'm glad I have the means to support my family the way I do."

"I see." He shook his head, his eye for a moment caught by some movement outside the window. I felt an inkling of annoyance, but remained unsure of why. This old man was merely trying to be helpful. His naivety was apparent.

"Shah," I continued. "I appreciate the gesture. I really do, but I just don't have the time to do something like this. I could probably arrange a donation to the camp or something like that."

"This is not for them," he snapped, with a sudden sharpness in his voice. "It is for you."

"I don't understand." There it is again.

"What do you strive for in your job?"

Leaning back, I stretched my arms behind my head and laced my fingers together. My gaze drifted up towards the ceiling. "I guess I strive to do what I'm supposed to do. What's expected of me and a little bit more than that. It is how I've moved forward, after all."

"Yes, you strive for results."

"Naturally. How else do you think I became the youngest employee vetted for the VP position within the company?"

"Let me ask you another question. That little boy, the one who fell in love with those horses so long ago, what do you think he would say if he met you today?"

It took me a moment to understand his meaning, until the tumblers turned and fell into place in my mind. "Look Shah," I began. "That little boy couldn't have had any idea what kind of responsibilities a person would be faced with throughout life. I was a child who saw something beautiful and powerful and felt drawn to it. That's all."

"You say that as if it is of no consequence."

"It is of no consequence," I replied.

"As a father, is this what you hope to teach your children?" Shah questioned, as he leaned back in his chair and rubbed his palm over the raspy flesh at his chin. I knew he was not yet finished making his point.

"Well, isn't it?" I threw back at him, leaning my elbows on my knees and waiting for his response.

"You are striving for results instead of striving for expression. This leads to empty success."

"What is empty success?" It was all I could do not to roll my eyes.

"Spreadsheets, finance reports. None of that brings joy to your soul. That is empty success. You work for someone else and not for you. You do not strive for aligned performance."

"Okay." I said with a sigh. I didn't have anything left in me to argue with him and, in a strange way, his words made sense. They might not apply to me necessarily, but they made sense.

"Would you like some tea?" he asked, pushing against the arms of the chair to lift himself to his feet. He puttered over to the stove and reached for the kettle. I was amused at his tendency to jump from deep philosophical discussions to something as simple as making tea. The rest of the afternoon, I knew, would consist of commenting on nothing greater than the events happening just outside the window, birds, squirrels, breezes in the leaves.

"Tea would be nice," I replied, letting a sigh of relief escape.

***

The following days consisted of much to do with reorganizing my office, and making sure I had the appropriate key cards and access codes for the official promotion coming up.

"As soon as the paperwork goes through," Benjamin said. "We can get you going. I tell you, I'm going to have a lot more free time once you step up, Kumar." He gave a hearty chuckle from behind his desk. I sat across from him in his office, listening. "Anytime, Kumar, anytime you have a question or you need anything, my door is open."

"Of course," I replied. "I do have one question if you have time."

He motioned for me to continue, glancing back to make sure the door was closed between us and Cynthia, who was keeping her post.

"You have mentioned," I began. "How your time will free up after I step into the VP position. What do you mean by that?"

He considered my words for a moment, glancing towards the thickly curtained window at the edge of his office. "I like to think of myself as a human animal, Kumar."

"Can you explain that?" I asked, propping my ankle up onto my knee. If I had learned anything during my time here it was that, Benjamin could spin a yarn when he wanted to. This moment had all the earmarks of him doing so.

"I think so," he replied, leaning back in his chair. "As the human animal it is our responsibility to feed, not only to keep ourselves alive, but to strive towards finding our own happiness."

"What makes you happy, if I may ask, Mr. Benjamin."

"Please, by this point you should call me Frank."

"Alright then," I said. The idea felt foreign, but I knew he would insist until I did so. "Frank."

"Kumar, I want you to think about my life for a moment. To think about where I started…not much different from you. I started at the bottom and worked my way up the ladder. And now, not only am I at the *top* of the ladder, but I *own* the ladder. Having you coming on as VP will allow me to take advantage of some of the investment opportunities which have come my way. I'll have more time to expand my portfolio."

"What would that accomplish?" I asked. "I'm not trying to be rude or nosy. But I am curious."

"I want more," he replied with a surprised tone. "I want to see how much I can do in my lifetime. How much money I can accumulate. Just like a bear putting away for the winter. You can never have enough. But to answer your question, my current worth is sitting at about fifteen million. My hope is to double that within three years' time."

"What are you going to do with it, Frank? All that money?"

"Do? I don't plan on doing anything with it!" he answered, incredulously.

"What about charities? You could do a lot of good with that much money."

He waved his hands as if swatting away a fly. "Bah!

Charities are a bunch of nonsense. I'm not into that. I'm doing it for me."

"I see," I replied, nodding my head and feeling a bit of disappointment, deep down.

"Don't be fooled, Kumar. They say that money cannot buy happiness, but I'm here to tell you that there is nothing better than a fat, juicy steak, the finest champagne, the taste of caviar bursting on the tongue..." His eyes went distant and a smile drifted across his face. "I like the finer things in life. I'm not going to lie. I've worked hard to get here and I don't apologize for enjoying my creature comforts."

I nodded, without giving a response, internally rolling his words around in my head.

"Animals, Kumar," he said catching my gaze. "Never forget that's what we are. That's all we are."

"You give me a lot to think about, Frank," I replied.

He grinned and shook his head, his voice booming with laughter. "I would hope so, Kumar! I would hope so!"

I stood and exited the office, giving a wave to Cynthia as I passed by her desk. She nodded and tapped on the headset, indicating she was in the middle of a phone call.

***

"Something seems to be bothering you today, Kumar." Shah observed, as he sat serenely in his print chair, hands crossed and elbows leaning on the padded arms.

"I don't know," I said, glancing out the window at the park. "I just don't think it's responsible for him to have that much money and not help anyone with it."

"Why do you think he is not helping anyone?" Shah raised his eyebrows.

"He said so himself. He's not giving anything to charity. His whole goal is to feed the 'animal', so to speak."

"Ah." Shah leaned forward and sipped his tea, lifting it carefully from the side table. "And what do you think that means?"

"He said, that we are basically human animals. That our instincts are in place to keep us alive."

"Do you disagree with this?"

"Well, no. I mean he's right on a very basic level."

"Yes…but?" The china cup clinked as he placed it back in the saucer.

"But what?" I asked.

"That which separates us from the other animals is the ability to think about what we think."

Here we go, I thought. "Alright. I'll bite. What do you mean by that?"

"The ability to stop and think. That's the defining factor between every other mammal and humans. Meta-cognitive response."

"Meta-cognitive?" I shook my head.

"The ability to think about your thoughts."

"Meaning what, exactly?"

"Your friend, Mr. Benjamin, seems to pursue things that make him feel good. Would you say that is true?"

"That's fairly accurate, yes," I replied, nodding my head in agreement.

"What he does not understand is that pain is good sometimes. We cannot feel good at all times."

"Wait," I said holding up my hands before me. "Pain is *good*? I've followed you so far, but just how do you work out that pain is good?"

He pushed himself to his feet, took hold of his cane,

something he had been using more frequently as of late, and hobbled across the room towards me. For a moment, I thought he would sit down on the couch next to me; but he paused before me, lifted his cane and brought the tip of it down onto my toes. Hard.

"What the hell!" I responded, leaping to my feet as pain shot up my ankle.

"There you see?" Calmly and without emotion he returned to his chair, propping his arm upon the chair.

"See what?" I seethed, feeling genuinely pissed off.

"The pain communicated that there was a stick bearing down upon your foot. If you had not moved out of the way, the pressure could have damaged your foot. The pain, in this case was good for you."

Begrudgingly, I took my seat again, rubbing the top of my shoe with my fingers.

Chapter Nine

"What you get by achieving your goals is not as important as what you become by achieving your goals."
–Zig Ziglar

On my first day as VP, I awoke as the sun rose and took a walk around the block. My nerves buzzed, waiting for 7 o'clock to arrive, and I needed to expel some excited energy before the workday began.

My toe still pulsed from Shah's lesson, the stinging reminder of his words about the benefits of pain. I passed by a homeless man, sitting outside a convenience store, his back parked against the store's display for cheap beer and cigarettes.

"You got a quarter, bro?" he asked me.

I raised my hands and shrugged, avoiding eye contact, hoping that he wouldn't sense that my pocket contained a billfold holding at least a hundred dollars. I passed by, unscathed.

Shah said that one had to feel pain in order to feel relief, that pain prevented us from further injury. I justified my lie to the homeless man, figuring that the pain he experienced would eventually dissipate into happiness. In a way, I did him a favor. Feeding him money would have only made him crave more. What kind of a lesson is that?

I left a few minutes before seven, unable to wait any longer. I bounded into my office, alert after two strong cups of coffee. My desk sat like a monument to my new position, announcing that I'd finally made it. The pristine oak glistened, from the sun's rays pouring from the windows, and invited me to have a seat.

I plumped down on the softest leather I'd ever felt. I spun around once, twice, then returned to my empty desk, ready for whatever would be thrown my way.

Frank told me he'd be in at eight to go through the day's tasks. Yet 8:30 rolled around and Frank was nowhere to be seen. Instead, Cynthia lumbered into the office with a stack of documents the size of a large child. She didn't look quite awake.

"Good morning Cynthia," I beamed, trying out my official VP voice, which was an octave or two lower than my normal speaking voice.

"Hi Kumar," she said. "Mr. Benjamin won't be in today so I'm here to get you up to speed."

"Where is he?" I asked. I was eager for Frank to see me, officially occupying my new throne.

"Not sure," she said, buckling under the weight of the documents. "He may be in later, but you never know with Mr. Benjamin."

"No problem," I said. "So what's on the docket today?"

She slammed the documents on my desk. "Mr. Benjamin needs you to peruse these files. They're investment opportunities for the upcoming fiscal year."

I peeked at the top page, which read, "Airtech Prospectus."

"Easy stuff," I replied, with a wave of my hand. "I can have these done by noon. That's it?"

Cynthia looked uneasy. "Well no, that's not it. You'll probably need to get through those quicker. Here's your meeting schedule for the day."

She slapped down a single mimeograph sheet, filled to the margins with names and times.

"This is for the week?" I asked, in disbelief.

"For *today*," she said.

My eyes bulged. "How am I supposed to meet with *this* many people? Three minutes per interview? We'll still be doing small talk!"

"Then skip the small talk," she said with a grin.

I pointed to one cluster of names. "Look, here it has me meeting *two* people at *once*? Am I supposed to *clone* myself?"

She shrugged. "I'm just the messenger." She left me alone with my mountain of documents.

I started to sweat. I hadn't quite realized that a doubling of salary meant a doubling of work. But this was more like a quintupling of work.

Frank hardly ever appeared flustered. He kept a jovial demeanor, as if he'd just returned from 18 holes of golf. How did he manage not to jump out the window with this much stuff to do?

I rubbed my eyes, shook out my wrists and repeated "Okay" for a few minutes, trying to compose myself.

***

A half-hour through the morning, and I'd already burned through a quarter of the prospectus. The documents contained a random assortment of start-ups, from AI-assisted toll booth operators to a business providing entertainment for infants. I passed on almost all of them, failing to see how this related to life insurance.

But one stood out to me. It was a company named "Pain Is Gain," with the logo of a fist occupying the center of a smiling mouth. I skimmed through their financial forecasts, which looked modest but promising, considering the unique idea. Pain Is Gain offered their clients a terrifying scenario, such as being dropped into a pit of simulated snakes. The object was to escape the room by working with your team.

The company described its philosophy. "We believe that fear and pain unite us as a people. As we cling to our peer's support through the most stressful of times, we find a deeper connection through the link of suffering."

Their mission statement brought to mind Shah's words and the surprise poke to my foot. I placed Pain Is Gain into my "Approved" pile and glanced at my watch. I was already ten minutes late to my first meeting with the art department.

I grabbed my jacket and jogged down the hall to the conference room. I took a minute to fix my hair, then entered. Two young men and a woman all stashed their phones as I walked through the door, like high schoolers seeing the principal enter the classroom. I exuded a false sense of confidence, with wide strides and an even wider smile.

This was my first entrance as VP, after all.

I sensed nervousness among the group as I went around shaking hands. Was I really causing this discomfort? This ability to affect their psyche made me feel powerful for the first time. Rather than be reprimanded for being late, I was rewarded with fear.

"Welcome everyone," I announced. I almost apologized for being late, but thought better of it. "We only have a couple minutes so let's move through this quick."

Danny, looking fresh out of college with greasy black hair and scars bearing the evidence of teenage acne, spoke first. "Sir—err, Mr. V.P."

"Call me---Mr. Vedig please."

"Mr. Vedig," he stammered, "we prepared the vector mapping for the web ads. It's not done yet. We still need to tweak some last minute compositing, but you'll get the main idea."

I nodded along, as if I knew what vector mapping or compositing were.

James, the other guy in the room, typed on his laptop while Susan, the woman, plugged in the projector's AV cable into the side of the computer.

I looked at my watch. Already three minutes over. Unintentionally, my glance sent the group scurrying even faster.

"How long is this?" I asked.

"Only a minute or two," Danny yelped.

"Okay we just need to be aware of the time," I said. *Because I wasn't aware of the time*, I wanted to add.

They all nodded in unison. Susan pointed a remote at the projector, revealing a scene of a skyscraper. Danny loudly hit a key on his laptop and the video started playing. The video showed a towering skyscraper, shaking, then finally buckling under its own weight.

"The narration will go under this part," Jamey said nervously. They all watched for my reaction, clues to decipher what I felt. I tried to hold as a neutral face as possible as the skyscraper eventually toppled to the ground into pieces. The pieces reassembled themselves into the Green Point logo.

"Looks good," I said, slowly nodding.

"That's it?" Billy asked. Evidently, I was expected to provide constructive feedback.

"Do you think it's too negative?" Susan asked.

"Now that you mention it," I said slowly, cocking my head to one side. "Perhaps we don't want our company to be associated with a collapsed building. Come back in two weeks and we'll see what you come up with."

"Two weeks?" Billy asked, an edge in his voice.

"Yes," I replied.

"But the project is supposed to be submitted this week."

"Okay, then make it two days," I said.

"You want us to create a new campaign in two days?"

"It can be done," I said, confidently.

I witnessed sweat forming on the brows of the three employees. I took joy in causing not only an emotional, but now a physical reaction as well.

They jumped out of their seats in panic, nodded at me, then darted out of the room.

That was easy, I thought. And only took fifteen minutes.

On and on this went for the next five hours. I met with finance managers, human resources, the web team. Every meeting ended with my request to meet again in a couple days. I thought I had found the secret to managing the intense workload.

The meetings were finished around four, when I was finally able to hunker down and delve back into the pile of prospectus.

Barely a page in, I heard Frank's boisterous voice echo through the halls. He entered my office like a hurricane with a huge grin, his skin lightly crisped from afternoon golf.

"Hey there kid," he said, "how did it go?"

"Um, okay," I said. "I didn't realize how many meetings there would be."

"Ahh," he said with a dismissive wave. "I usually

cancel half of them anyway. You met with everyone?"

"Every single one," I said through gritted teeth.

"Kumar, you need to realize that *you're* in charge now," Frank said. "You don't answer to *them*. They answer to *you*. If you're overwhelmed, you have the ability to cancel."

"But then I'm just piling more on my plate for later."

"Let me let you in on a little secret," he said, leaning in. "Most of these meetings are pointless, simply a courtesy. And you're being paid too much to be courteous. You earned your keep. Now use it."

"But won't cancelling affect the company?" I asked.

"Most of these guys will figure it out on their own," Frank said, waving his hand in dismissal. "Allow them the freedom."

"The freedom to be *confused*?"

"No, the freedom to discover their own path. How much did you actually accomplish in these meetings?"

I thought about it. "Not much, I guess. I didn't even know what half of them were talking about."

"*Exactly*," he said with a wink. "This is the half that you cancel. What do you know about art or advertising?"

"Nothing," I replied.

"So let the art and advertising guys pick up the tab. Remember Kumar, money isn't about buying things. It's about power. Power is choice, being able to decide where and when you want to do something."

"Okay," I said, "I guess I just need to get used to having a choice."

"Wait until you see your first paycheck," he said, his grin widening. "Trust me, you've got a *lot* of choice." I cocked an eyebrow, intrigued and he continued on. "So let's *choose* to celebrate. Tino's?"

I patted my stack of documents. "I would love to, but I've got *these* to sift through."

Frank picked up the documents and placed them on a chair. "And now they're gone. See how easy that was?"

"But—"

"They'll be there when we get back. What's your choice?"

***

In the blink of an eye, I found myself sitting in front of a piping hot porterhouse, paired with a stein of strong IPA.

Frank finished a story about a sky gliding incident in Cabo. "The guy paid $10,000 to break his leg!" he said with a chuckle. I laughed along, although I'd only half listened.

"I wanted to ask you about the prospectus," I said.

Frank's smile grew smaller, barely perceptible. "See any good one's in there?"

"A few. Well, one in particular. But what's it for? These startups have nothing to do with Green Point," I said.

"They have nothing to do with Green Point *as it stands*. Very astute."

"Then why—"

"Do you know the worst thing a business can do?" he interrupted.

"What?"

"Stand still," he said. "The world we live in moves so fast. Those who aren't ready to adapt will die. It's survival of the fittest."

"What are we adapting to?" I asked. "Are you saying that Green Point won't be dealing in life insurance anymore?"

"We're going to become whatever we need to become in order to grow," he said.

"But why not concentrate on building up our customer base? We already have a specialty."

"What if Apple decided to stick with only making personal computers? Or how about if Xerox ignored the marketplace and continued to focus on copy machines? Would they still be around?"

"No, probably not," I admitted.

"Definitely not," he said, vigorously. "It's not enough to be the best at what you do anymore. The world changes so much that we need to change with it. We need to embrace chaos, Kumar."

"I know a thing or two about chaos," I said out of the corner of my mouth.

"Then you'll do just fine," he said, his smile returning.

***

Frank dropped me off at the office a little before 10 pm. I felt slightly buzzed and exhausted. Just as I exited the car, he called after me.

"I need about twenty of those prospectuses analyzed by tomorrow. How much did you get done?"

"At least twenty," I said, avoiding eye contact—the old liar's tool. I'd really only gotten through less than ten.

Frank threw me a wink and tore off into the night, leaving me with at least four hours of work.

***

Nikki was still awake when I got home. I tiptoed into the house, as if I'd snuck out for the evening. Fortunately, I was met with a sweet smile and a sweeter kiss.

"How was your first day, hotshot?" Nikki asked, sweetly.

"Busy," I huffed. "Sorry I'm so late. Frank needed me—"

"I figured you'd be late," she said. "With your first day and all."

"After this week, things will go back to normal. I'll be out of the office by six."

"Make breakfast for the kids in the morning and we'll be square."

"Deal," I agreed, offering her a smile.

"I was going to bed, but I'll stay up for a bit if you wanted to watch some TV."

"There's nothing I would love more," I said. "But I've got a little bit more work I need to ready for tomorrow."

Nikki's cheerful demeanor deflated into a weary frown. She didn't look bitter, or angry; just tired.

"Okay," she said. "I'm giving you a pass this week. Don't blow it."

"I know, I know," I said. "Like I said, next week, back to normal."

"Mmm," she responded. I detected more than a hint of skepticism. Yet, I was too tired, busy, and buzzed to start a fight right then. I let her go to bed with as soft a kiss that I could muster.

I combed through the pile of prospectus until the sun came up. It was one of those nights where you're not sure if you ever slept.

In the morning, I blasted out of bed, woke the kids, then prepared a breakfast that would make the Queen of England jealous. Omelets, french toast, pancakes, I went all out to show that I could not only juggle two worlds, but excel at doing so.

I watched as the kids dug into their morning feast, enjoying the silence that only a satisfying meal can create. I kissed them on their foreheads and headed to the office.

Once I got to the office, I was radiant—confident that I could handle the intense workload and a family life. Cynthia stopped me on my sprint into the office. She took one look at me and cringed. "Kumar, you look like Hell."

"Really?" I said, in disbelief. "I feel great!"

"Did you sleep?"

"I think so," I answered, hesitantly. "I'm not sure."

She shook her head. "Not good. As happy as you think you are, the bags around your eyes tell the real story."

"I just had a busy first day," I said. "I'll get some sleep tonight."

"She eyed me skeptically. "Don't let this job kill you, Kumar. We need you around here. If you need help, I'm always here."

"Thanks, I appreciate that," I said, slowly backing away toward my office, pile of documents in hand.

The flood of unread emails looked like I hadn't checked my inbox for weeks. But they were all from today. I opened a couple and answered back with a quick "yes" or "no" to the employee's mostly trivial questions.

I then remembered Frank's advice about setting the workers free. Replying to these emails would take me three hours, easy. Half my day would be gone. That's when I decided to set them free and ignore the rest of the emails.

Out of twelve meetings scheduled for the day, I cancelled six, again adhering to Frank's advice. To my delight, less meetings meant that I could take my time and focus on the department issues.

My first meeting was with Bill Tanner, VP of Marketing. He wanted to follow up about my notes on the collapsed building ad. Bill wasn't the small talk type and launched right into his concern. "My team tells me that you ordered an entirely new project."

"That's correct Mr. Tanner," I said. "Is this a problem?"

"Well yes, it actually is a huge problem," he said, leaning in toward me. "Those animators worked hard on the project."

"I just didn't think that a collapsed building—"

"Yes, my colleagues explained your concerns. I think you may have missed the point." I felt the defensive hairs crawl up my back as Tanner continued. "The ad isn't about a building collapsing. The collapse is a *metaphor*, of course, but you already knew that." He displayed a sly smile. "But it's deeper than a cheap metaphor. We used that image to tap into the most universal fear there is—the fear of death."

"I just think it might be a little much," I said dryly.

"It's too much for people to acknowledge death?" He waited for me to respond, but I stayed silent. "How do people die these days?"

I didn't answer, thinking it a rhetorical question. Then I saw Tanner's waiting gaze.

"Um, cancer, car accidents—"

"Exactly," he said. "To be exact, the order goes heart disease, cancer, and respiratory diseases. Yet how are most people afraid of dying?"

"Terrorism, I suppose," I responded, not sure where he was going with this.

"Bingo!" he said, raising his hand and pointing his index finger in the air. "Cancer isn't photogenic. Neither are respiratory diseases. But *terrorism* is tailor-made for a Hollywood blockbuster."

"I see," I said, only partly sure I understood. "Can I make a suggestion?" I asked.

Tanner looked uneasy. "Sure."

"Can we make it bigger? More impactful. I just didn't feel the emotion."

Tanner smiled and nodded his head. "I think we can handle that."

Chapter Ten

"Whenever you're in conflict with someone, there is one factor that can make the difference between damaging your relationship and deepening it. That factor is attitude."
—William James

For the first time as VP, I was challenged. Bill's game of mental chess invigorated me. The meetings no longer looked like burdens, but rather opportunities to develop my mental acumen.

I readied my revelation to share with Shah as I headed towards his apartment. The front door's glass reflected back a renewed Kumar. The bags disappeared, replaced by a wide-eyed readiness. I bounded up the stairs, like a kid about to tell his mom he got accepted to Harvard.

I heard Shah whisper behind the door. I tapped softly, then heard the groans of an old man getting out of his chair. He answered the door with a gentle smile that grew wider when he saw the vitality on my face.

"I take it your first days have seen you well," he asked, ushering me into his apartment.

"Yes, they have," I said, looking around as I took a seat on the couch. "More cats?"

A chocolate cat with a mangled tail emerged from under Shah's chair. Following the cat were three identical kittens.

"It appears that I have a weakness," he said with a smile, as he sat in his chair. "Tell me about your experiences so far."

"At first it was crazy. I was overwhelmed. It was...

chaos. But then I figured out how to prioritize my time and I felt like I got it down."

"And what is it that you're prioritizing?"

I thought about it. "People, I guess," I said. "I was buried in paperwork and put some of it aside. It opened up my day so I could get to more meetings."

Shah nodded. "Your meetings went well?"

"Yes," I nearly shouted. "My first few were a bit disappointing because they were meek. But today, there was a guy—Bill— who challenged me and I liked it."

"Because?" he motioned for me to continue.

"I guess it was the stimulation. It kept me on my toes, made me want to think faster."

"Is that all," he pried, "a game?"

"If you want to reduce it to that. I mean, life is one big challenge, right?"

"How do you win this game? Or, I'm sorry, *challenge*."

"What? When I...beat his argument, I suppose."

Shah shook his head. "What you felt today, what you enjoyed, was connecting with another human being. This challenge was really collaboration."

Shah gave one of the kittens a scratch while I prepared a rebuttal. "How could we be collaborating when we have opposing goals?" I asked.

"Oh, you have opposing goals? What is your goal?"

"To...create the best products we can."

"And his?" he asked.

I let his question linger in the air. He resumed. "It appears that your real goal is to gain power over this individual,"

"To a degree, yes," I admitted, avoiding eye contact. "But the only way a corporation can function is through hierarchy. I'm his superior for a reason."

"Are you?" he asked.

"What's your point?" I asked impatiently.

"Seek collaboration," he said, enfolding his fingers, "Connection. Acknowledge that you and he have the same objective. This is not a battle, but an alliance."

"I think I got you," I said.

"What was the discussion's outcome?"

"He explained how we were selling the fear of death—"

Shah laughed at the phrase and shook his head. "Go on," he said.

My voice grew aggravated. "He made a good case for the commercial. Then I made a decision to amplify the message to make it more…scary."

"So you took his idea?" he asked, raising his eyebrows.

"No," I snapped. "I expanded upon his previous concept."

"By copying it," he said. I shook my head silently. "I'm not accusing you," he said. "There's nothing wrong with your decision. Take a look at the kittens over there."

In the corner of the room, the kittens clumsily cleaned themselves with their paws. Beside them, their mother confidently combed her back legs with her teeth.

"They mimic their mother," Shah said. "Why?"

"Because it's their mother," I said.

"Do children always listen to their parents?"

"We both know the answer to that," I replied with a chuckle.

Shah laughed. "We mimic others when our survival depends on it. We learn coping skills from others."

"Bill isn't my dad," I said sourly.

Shah shook his head. "Humans are society's mirrors.

These mirrors enable us to reflect back on ourselves the actions and emotions of others. You have brain cells that remind you that you are not alone in the world. Perhaps you took Bill's idea because you admire him."

I watched the kittens continue to clean as the clock ticked away. After a few minutes of silence, I looked over at Shah and noticed he'd fallen asleep. I placed a blanket over his body and let myself out.

***

After leaving Shah's, I avoided the office and headed straight home. Nikki fell back on the couch in surprise, looking at the clock. "Wow, so early," she said.

"7 o'clock," I said. "That's normal for most people."

Her face lit up. My body buzzed at seeing the happiness on her face. The kids ran out and grabbed onto my legs, shouting incoherently in joy.

"Go wash up guys," Nikki said to the kids. "We get to eat with daddy tonight!"

The kids bounded off. We heard the slam of the bathroom door. Nikki smiled. "Maybe I was wrong about you taking the position."

I wanted to scream, *Yes, you were wrong!* But I restrained myself. Shah said this wasn't a challenge. I decided to collaborate.

At dinner, I couldn't help but feel like an invited guest. It was clear that I broke the normal dynamic of dinner table etiquette, an observation that forced me to realize just how absent I'd been.

"Danny rescued Sandra today," Jillian said in the middle of a biteful of chicken.

Nikki over exaggerated a surprised response. I looked around the table. "Who's Danny, honey?" I asked. "A friend?"

Jillian looked at me as if I'd asked her if water was wet. Her scrunched up expression told me not to ask anything further.

"It's from her stupid show," Khan spat before burying his face in a bottle of Gatorade.

"It's not stupid!" Jillian yelled back.

Nikki extended her hands like a referee. I'd become powerless in negotiating peace between my children. All I could do was simply stare at each of their faces in abject horror. Nikki extinguished the situation and calmly spoke to me.

"Danny is a *hippo*," she said.

I must have looked confused because she continued.

"He's a hippo that's best friends with Sandra, the *giraffe*."

"In Africa," Jillian clarified.

"In Africa," Nikki agreed.

"It's from one of her shows?" I asked.

Now Nikki gave me the same bewildered look as Jillian. "Yeah," she said. "It's not real."

I finished the rest of my meal in silence as the kids hollered about things that I didn't understand.

***

Perhaps it was due to the comfort of enjoying a normal night's sleep beside my wife that I overslept the next morning. I couldn't remember hitting snooze, but my phone indicated that I'd delayed my wakeup no less than eight times. I awoke in a panic, jumping out of bed like a soldier off to war.

Not having enough time to make breakfast, I left out two Pop Tarts and a note reading, "Sorry," accompanied by a frowny face.

No one seemed to notice that I was late as I shuffled through the halls and into my office. Once in my office, the world piled its problems directly onto my back. A frantic series of emails from Frank greeted me. Each one grew in anxiety as Frank demanded to know whether I'd gotten through the prospectus.

Through all my efforts of trying to balance my day, I'd neglected to go through the rest of the documents. They laid, untouched, on my desk, mocking me.

I tried to get hold off Frank, responding that I'd be done by noon. I poured through the documents like a madman, trying to discover a government conspiracy. At 12:01, Frank appeared at my door, looking uncharacteristically worried.

"Please tell me you're done," he said.

Luckily, I was putting the finishing touches on the last prospectus. I made a show of closing the final page. "All reviewed and evaluated," I said.

"You told me you would have these done two days ago," he said. "What happened?"

"I took your advice," I said, lightly smiling. "I'm trying not to let this job kill me."

"My advice was to miss deadlines?" Frank's frown quickly wiped the smile off my face.

"No, but I needed to take the meetings and—"

Frank put up his hand. "If you don't complete tasks on time, then why should anyone below you finish on time? You're supposed to be a role model, Kumar."

"I'm sorry sir. It was just…the dinner the other night. It was late."

"It was late?" he said incredulously. "That's exactly what I'm trying to avoid—being late."

"I don't get why these are so important," I said.

"Do I need to explain it to you again?"

"No sir," I said, beginning to perspire. "But I thought the current campaigns were more important."

"See?" he said. "Kumar, you're too invested in the present. You need to be looking toward the future."

He reached into a briefcase and pulled out a stack of documents. He slapped them on my desk. "This is the future," he said. "I need these done by tomorrow."

"I'm on it Frank," I said. "Don't you worry."

"Oh I never *worry*," Frank said with a smile.

The week flew by in a blur. I felt like I hadn't been living so much as standing still while life whirled around me. Most of my time was spent hunched over the documents, checking and rechecking my numbers, only taking time out to answer the constant stream of emails. The "ding" of a new email became the soundtrack to my frustration. My hand felt cramped, my mind felt like melted plastic.

I arrived home regularly past midnight, creeping into bed next to my sleeping wife. Other nights, I stuck it out on the couch, fearful of another oversleeping episode.

By the end of the week, I craved Shah like a kid craves ice cream.

***

That Friday, I arrived early at Shah's apartment, pacing his stoop for a few minutes before entering. I didn't want him to see me in full freakout mode.

My attempts at masking my pain must have failed because the first words out of Shah's mouth upon seeing me were, "Uh, oh."

"What?" I replied, walking into his apartment.

"You don't look so good."

"Tough week," I said, shrugging my shoulders as I took my regular place on the couch.

"They're all tough weeks if you approach life with the wrong attitude. Explain to me what happened." Shah gracefully walked over to his chair and sat, waiting for my response.

"I thought I had it figured out, then Frank Benjamin dumped an impossible amount of work for me to complete. It's like he's trying to kill me."

"Tasks to finish?"

"Yes," I replied.

"There's your problem," he said, leaning back in his chair.

I cocked a confused eyebrow. Shah continued. "You're looking at these tasks as something to finish rather than a process to aid your growth, to learn from."

"How can I grow when Benjamin gives me more than I can handle?"

"Have you said no to any of his requests?" he asked.

"No." I stated, amused that Shah even asked that question.

"Why?" he asked.

"Why?" I repeated, the desperation oozing from my voice. "I'll be fired and sent back to be a quant."

"Are you sure about that?"

"Pretty sure, yeah," I said.

"Are you happier now than when you were a quant?"

"No, not really," I admitted.

Shah paused, nodding slowly. "You blame Benjamin, yet you're not being honest with him. You're also not being honest with yourself."

"But he's the one making my life miserable," I insisted.

Shah shook his head. "No, it is *you* who are making your life miserable and making it more difficult than it needs to be."

"You don't understand," I said, shaking my head.

"Do you believe that I've never struggled?" Shah leaned forward, with his hands on his knees.

"I'm sure you have," I said, feeling a bit guilty. But the guilt calmed me down. "Sometimes I wish I were selling hot dogs in the park."

"I can have that arranged," he said, smiling.

I laughed. "No thanks. So, what do I do?"

"First off, stop blaming Benjamin. If the work is overwhelming, tell him the truth; that you can't handle it. Often people are more compassionate than you would think."

"Okay, I think I can do that," I said.

"Next, you need to approach your work in a different paradigm. Appreciate the process of what you're doing. Stop thinking about the end result. This will allow you to enter the state which we refer to as aligned."

"Which is?" I asked.

"When you are aligned, your energy just takes over. It won't feel like you're working anymore, but rather that it's an automatic process, like breathing."

"How do I become aligned?"

"By ridding your thoughts of the need for results and instead giving yourself over to the process of your mission.

Results will never bring you happiness, but will only leave you craving more." Shah got up and walked over to his desk. Picking up a pen, he scribbled on a small notepad.

"I need more time," I said in defeat.

Shah looked up from his notepad. "Ahh, but time is a mere illusion, Kumar. If you had thirty hours in a day, you would simply add six hours of new tasks." He resumed writing. "Stop obsessing about time."

"What are you writing?"

Shah stopped writing, tore a small slip of paper from his notepad and handed it to me. I glanced at the paper, which contained a list of seemingly random tasks. "What's this?" I asked him.

"This is a list of tasks I'd like you to complete by the end of the day," he said.

"Let me get this straight," I said. "You're helping me deal with being overworked by giving me *more* work?"

"This isn't work. And you're not overworked. You're going about your work in the wrong way."

"What's the right way?" I asked, incredulously.

"Embrace the process. Enjoy the journey regardless of the destination."

"So you're saying I don't really have to complete these?" I questioned, holding the piece of paper in the air.

"No, I'm saying that if you give yourself over to the process, you'll complete them, whether you plan to or not."

I looked at the list. "Bring firewood to the North Bank? It's dangerous."

"Why is it dangerous?" he asked.

"I could be robbed," I replied.

"For your wood? You're giving it to them anyway. Why would they steal it from you?"

I tried to think of a comeback but couldn't. Shah looked at the clock on the wall. "You can start now," he said.

"Great," I said, deflated.

***

The first task instructed me to "Get a carrot cake donut from Do-Rite and return." I started toward the subway, but stopped after a few steps. It didn't make any sense to tackle that one first. The donut would melt by the time I got back. Besides, Shah could wait for his donut.

"Why am I doing this?" I asked myself, looking back at the list.

I decided on the second task, where I was to "Plant 10 sweet lemon trees in the courtyard." I had never heard of a sweet lemon, never mind the fact that I had no idea where to find one.

I checked four different grocery stores, receiving only blank looks when I asked for sweet lemon seeds. One kid, an acne infested teenager, grabbed a regular lemon off the shelf and held it up, as if I didn't know what a lemon was.

I hobbled back towards Shah's apartment, already defeated by the first task. A few blocks from Shah's place, I came across a Middle Eastern market and went inside. The market was barren of customers. Goods scattered the shelves in no particular order. Boxes were stacked in the middle of the aisles.

A short Middle-Eastern man emerged from behind a curtain in the back, wearing a huge grin. "Hello, my friend," he said, greeting me like royalty.

"Hi, this might be a weird question, but do you have sweet lemon seeds?"

His eyes lit up. He waved into a back room, where one wall was filled with packets of seeds. "My family grew these in Iran," he said, grabbing a packet. "These are my favorite. I can relive childhood with these." He handed me the packet.

I continued back to Shah's to plant the seeds. Then I realized that I would need to chop the wood too. No sense in making two trips, I thought, and bought five cords of wood. A small, red wheelbarrow waited for me in the courtyard, presumably supplied by Shah.

For the next three hours, time disappeared as I got my hands filthy planting the seeds and spreading some mulch that I grabbed along the way. Once finished, I stood back and admired my handiwork. My hands, back, and legs ached, but in the way muscles ache after a good workout.

I felt good.

Chopping the wood presented a bit more difficulty, as I'd never done anything of the sort. Luckily, a neighbor named John saw me struggling and offered his help. I saw John's smooth strokes as he repeated the same angle each time he came down with the axe.

"How do you know where to come down on the wood?" I asked John.

"Instinct and a lot of practice," he said, spitting a glob of saliva to the ground. "Once you hit it just right, you'll know."

It was embarrassing to fail in front of John. My first few attempts sent chips of wood splintering away, the log still intact. John adjusted my hand position. I felt like a kid playing t-ball again.

"Stop thinking so much about it," he said. "Let your body take over, like dancing."

I closed my eyes and let it rip. When I opened my eyes, the wood sat in two symmetrical pieces, like an open melon. John gave me a high five.

"What are you doing this for anyway?" he asked.

"It's complicated, but I'm supposed to bring these to the North Bank."

"Right on, man," John said, nodding his head. "I'll join you if you don't mind. It's not the best area."

So, John joined me on my travels to the North Bank. His husky body put my mind at ease. A community of tents greeted us as we rolled the wheelbarrow over the grass. We got a few suspicious looks when we entered, but we were mostly ignored by the homeless residents of the camp.

"Where are we supposed to bring these," John asked.

"I'm not sure," I replied, glancing around, noticing the night settling in over the camp.

Just then, I smelt the sweet, stinging aroma of a burning fire. John and I followed the scent, which led to an outpost of burning barrels. Guys huddled around the fire on the cool night, warming their hands.

I steered the wheelbarrow up to where a small pile of wood was stacked. A balding man wearing a leather jacket approached. This guy was one you would not want to meet in a dark alley. But any fear was dispelled with his warm smile. He introduced himself as Butch and offered a firm handshake.

"You must be Shah's friend," Butch said.

"Yes, and this is for you," I said, placing down the wheelbarrow.

"Appreciate it," he said, pulling the wheelbarrow closer and throwing two logs into the fire.

With the mission accomplished, I checked off the first

task, Then I realized I could knock off two at once. "Butch, I have a weird question for you," I said.

"Anything boss," he said, turning around and smiling.

"What are you most afraid of?"

I would have expected a man in Butch's position to respond with death, violence, or maybe the fear of never having a stable home.

Butch looked to the sky. "My biggest fear?" he repeated. "It's that people will stop caring about me."

"Really?" I said, surprised by his answer.

"Absolutely," he said. "I can handle the tough stuff out here. But I can't handle it alone."

We shook hands and I left the park. John took a subway to the west side, wishing me well on whatever journey I was on.

With the more challenging tasks out of the way, I only needed to grab the coveted donut at Do-Rite. The excited cashier handed me the carrot cake delicacy with the care of a loving mother.

Back at Shah's, I reached the top stair and discovered a note on the door. "Treat yourself," the note read.

I sat outside on the stoop and munched on the most delicious treat I've ever consumed. I smiled toward the full moon as the sweetness enveloped my taste buds.

***

I approached the next morning with the goal of focusing on the process, rather than the result of my efforts. This proved to be more difficult, when assessing complicated financial documents, than it was to plant trees or eat donuts.

After a few hours, the numbers swirled around my head

like waking nightmares. I took a walk outside to clear my mind. Outside the office, I ran into Frank, who stepped out of his new silver Aston Martin, the car looking out of place in this neighborhood, or any neighborhood for that matter.

"We back on track, Kumar?" he asked me.

"Um yeah, it's going," I responded, weakly.

"That doesn't sound too confident."

"I should be honest with you."

"Yes you should," he said.

"These investment portfolios are killing me. I barely see my family because I'm here all night. I've tried so hard to handle it, but—" I let my words drift away. I waited for Frank to crush me.

"I'm not looking to *kill* you, Kumar. From the moment I met you, I saw a fire inside of you, something I rarely see in the guys that come through."

"Thank you sir," I said. *But you're fired*, is what I heard in my head.

"You don't just do this for the money. You genuinely want to win, and that's important in our world."

"I agree."

"But maybe I've been a bit unfair to you. I threw you into the fire, as they say," he admitted. "Do you know what drives a man Kumar?"

"Family?"

"Nope."

"Love?"

"No, but they're part of it. Incentives drive men. Incentives provide motivation, whether the incentive is love, sex, money, whatever. What will I gain from this? We may not admit it, but this is the only question that matters. Ask me." Frank looked at me in anticipation.

"Wh-what will I gain from this?" I stammered.

"Good question," he said. "I think you're lagging behind on these reports because there's no incentive for you."

"Maybe, but—"

"So here's what I'm going to do for you," he said, before I could finish my sentence. "I'll give you 15% equity in the investments you pick."

My eyes widened. "Really? That's very generous sir."

"Yeah it is. Because I'm a generous guy and because you deserve it. Plus, it'll keep you more engaged. It's a win-win. Deal?"

I said "yes" before I could even think about it.

Chapter Eleven

*"Focus on the journey, not the destination. Joy is found
not in finishing an activity but in doing it."*
–Greg Anderson

Evaluating investments became an obsession. I monitored stock prices as if my life depended on it. The rise and fall of share price matched my emotions, which escalated and deflated based on the company's standing. By the end of the day, the stock tracking exhausted my brain, the stimulation leaving me numb.

I forced myself out of the office around seven because my heart felt like it would pop out of my chest. I figured a meal with the family would calm my nerves.

Again, I felt as though I didn't belong in my house. I tried to trap inside the bitterness, the knowledge that I'd provided all of this, only to be ignored.

"Hey mom, what color is seven?" Khan asked his mother.

Nikki laughed. I had no idea what that meant.

"How high is a pound?" Jillian asked. The kids and Nikki laughed hysterically. Obviously, this was an inside joke. I was determined to get inside and tried my own.

"How many degrees is Poland?" I asked. The kids stared at me gravely.

"That doesn't work," Khan said.

"Mind your own business, daddy," Jillian said.

"Honey!" Nikki yelled at her. Jillian muttered to herself, while Khan laughed.

I shoveled spoonful's of mashed potatoes into my mouth, looking for an exit.

While Khan laughed, his body shook so hard that he knocked a glass of juice off the table. The smashing sent a tingling, high-frequency jolt to my insides. And I snapped.

"Go to your room!" I yelled.

"But I—" Khan protested.

"Hon—" Nikki tried to calm me down.

"Get...to...your...room now!" My nostrils flared. I scared myself, never before having lost control to this degree.

Khan went to his room sobbing and so did everyone else. I was left with a kitchen table full of uneaten food.

***

The dinner incident should have sounded alarms in my head to slow down. Unfortunately, my first paycheck was deposited into my bank account that morning, wiping away any sense of caution in my mind.

I stared at my account balance in wonder. I had to look at the screen three times to confirm that it was real.

On the way to Shah's, I wandered the streets like a man in love. A dumb smile was plastered on my face, which made passersby smile in return.

"You got paid today, didn't you?" Shah asked, barely letting me settle in my spot on the couch.

"Yeah," I said, feeling the smile stretch even further across my face. "How did you know?"

"I can read it on your face. The expression of an obsessive is unmistakable."

"I'm just happy is all," I responded, as I watched him sitting down his in chair.

"Are you?"

"Sure," I said. "I finally have something to show for all the hard work I've put in."

"Is this why you work hard? To have something to show for it?"

I frowned. "You really know how to rain on a parade, Shah."

"I'm afraid you haven't been listening to me."

"But I have!" I nearly cut him off. "I focused more on the process. That's how I was able to finish by deadline."

"You're still focusing on the reward, on the end result," he said, shaking his head.

"Am I supposed to just ignore the reward? Give it away?"

"Yes," he responded softly.

I waited for him to say more, but Shah just stared at me. "You're crazy," I said.

"Give 20% of your paycheck away for this week."

"And I repeat, you're crazy." I couldn't believe he was telling me to *give* away the money I had worked so hard to earn.

"If you truly want to untether your mind from the trap of material reward, you give half away."

"What if I don't want to?" I asked, admittedly sounding childish.

"Then that is your choice," he said. "And you will pay for that choice with the appropriate consequences."

"What kind of consequences?" I sat back, ready to hear what he would come back with.

"Misery, loneliness, confusion, to name a few."

"How do you know that?" I sneered.

"Do you think you're the first man to be paid well?

I've seen a generation of men just like you ruin themselves because of what you're feeling right now."

"I'm feeling like I'm winning." I leaned forward in excitement, trying to explain it to him.

"Exactly," he said. "You're stuck in a competition that you can never win."

I shook my head.

"How about this," Shah continued. "I *challenge* you to give 20% of your pay away."

I raised my head, my attention piqued. "You don't think I will?"

"I'm not sure if you're capable," he said.

I jumped out of my seat. "All right, we'll see," I said, heading for the door. "20% of this paycheck will be gone in three hours."

"Yes, we'll see," he said, as I walked out and shut the door behind me.

***

After leaving Shah's I dashed straight to the bank and withdrew three hundred dollars from the ATM. Sure, it wasn't half my pay, but I would complete this in steps. Besides, I was terrified, walking around with that much cash.

Since it was nearly Christmas, the Salvation Army people were outside the grocery store. I planned to drop at least a third of my cash in their bucket. I couldn't wait to see the Salvation Santa's eyes pop out of his head from my generosity.

I made a big show, strutting towards the bucket, swinging my keys. The bell's ring sounded less irritating than it usually did. I slowly pulled out my billfold and slid a hundred dollar bill in the bucket, as slowly as possible.

"Merry Christmas," the man said, making only brief eye contact. He continued to ring his bell. I stood around, waiting for more of a reaction. A woman sidled up behind me and dropped a dollar into the bucket.

"Merry Christmas," he repeated to the woman.

That's it? I thought to myself. *We get the same reaction?*

I trudged into the grocery store and bought myself a bottle of champagne to celebrate with Nikki.

On the way back to the car, I passed a bearded man with a ragged, light green jacket. I recognized him as the homeless guy I encountered at the convenience store a while back.

"You got any change, man?" he asked in the same cadence as before.

I flashed a smile at him. "It's your lucky day," I said, slapping a hundred dollar bill into his palm. His first instinct was to inspect it for forgery.

"Thanks, man," he said, beaming with joy.

It was then that I realized I had forgotten the champagne in the store. I jogged back, hoping that it hadn't been swiped in the meantime. It hadn't.

Heading back to my car with the champagne, the homeless man again asked me for change. "What do you mean?" I asked him, in disbelief. "I just gave you a hundred dollars!"

"Oh yeah," he said, flashing his yellowed teeth. "Have a good day."

I stood my ground. "Wait a minute," I said sternly. "You mean to tell me you *forgot* me after I just gave you a hundred bucks?"

He raised his hands and backed off. "Sorry man, bad memory," he said. "I was injured in Iraq." He pulled the hundred dollar bill out of his pocket and threw it in front of me. "I don't need your money."

"No, no, take it," I pleaded.

"I don't want it." He turned and walked away.

I debated leaving the money, but figured that it might blow away. I picked up the bill and stuffed it in my pocket. If I'd felt like I climbed a mountain that morning, by evening I felt like I was trapped in a mine shaft. I abandoned the charitable act, instead deciding that I could reward my family, an of act of charity in itself.

I stopped at the mall, where I went on a shopping spree worthy of a Kardashian. I loaded up on toys, kitchenware, clothes, house accessories, anything I could fit in a bag.

Trying to redeem the previous night, I bestowed my gifts upon the kids, making a presentation out of it. I received smiles all around, as the kids ran off to play with their toys. Nikki gave me a warm hug, then absconded to the bedroom, where she tried out her new tablet. They were happy. I was alone, but relieved.

***

My next appointment at Shah's came a week later. Since we'd last met, I continued my manic buying sprees, capping it off with a surprise trip to Maui, which I announced during dinner. I felt like a champion as I was rewarded with excited cheering. I was back in the club.

"I figured out how to balance the chaos," I told Shah, placing my cell phone on the table, as I sat on the couch.

"Oh, that's lovely to hear," he said. "Can you share your method?"

"It goes back to what you said about money; that it should be used as a tool, not as the endgame."

"Yes," he said. His voice betrayed a hint of skepticism.

"So I used my money as a tool," I said. "I haven't seen my family much so—I decided to spoil them. By *my* choice."

"I see," Shah said. "And how did that turn out?"

"Great, actually," I said, excitedly. "The kids were quiet all night. Nikki loved her tablet. Everybody was…happy."

"And today?"

"I haven't seen them today."

"Do you usually judge your children's happiness based on how quiet they are?" Shah questioned, as he reached up and rubbed his chin.

"No, but you know kids. When they're *really* into something, they're quiet."

"What do you think was the lesson in your act? From your children's perspective."

I felt myself growing defensive, a spike in my heart rate, the sign of a challenge. "It's that their father loves them very much and will do anything to make them happy."

"Anything, you say?"

"Anything." I stated, firmly.

"Would you give up your position?"

"I don't need to give it up, so that's irrelevant," I said, feeling disappointed in Shah's reaction. "You know, I was happy when I came in here. I'm starting to notice a pattern here."

"Happiness without fulfillment is simply consuming empty desires."

"Come again?"

"Your children will take an entirely different lesson

from this," Shah said. "They now associate your love with material things. What happens if you're no longer able to buy them things anymore?"

"I'll prevent that from happening."

"How?"

"By...working hard," I responded, not entirely confident.

Shah waved his hand towards me and said, "You already seem to be working hard."

"Okay, you're starting to aggravate me."

"Things change," he said. "That's the only constant. Order turns to chaos much more quickly than you'd like to believe."

"Ever the *optimist*," I said through the side of my mouth.

"If you couldn't buy them things, would they stop loving you? Or would they think that you've stopped loving them?"

"I don't know," I said, my voice drifting away.

"This is the trap you've set for yourself," he said, leaning in.

"So what do I do? Bring all the stuff back?"

"That won't be necessary. We can't change the past. But we can change the present."

"But I'm using money as a tool," I pleaded. "Like you said."

"No, you're using money as a bribe," he stated. "It becomes a false representation of love. A tool is used to assist you, not to deceive."

"I don't know. Your *lessons* haven't worked for me so far."

"Is that so?" he questioned, arching his eyebrow.

"No, like giving my money away? Terrible idea," I pointed out, defensively. "I ended up getting into a fight with a veteran over my money."

"Why?"

"I gave the guy money and he had the nerve to forget who I was."

"Did you give him the money so he'd remember you?"

"Well, not really," I said. "I guess I just wanted a positive reaction."

"You gave in order to get something."

"But something positive!" I protested. "I just wanted appreciation."

"And how would he have properly shown you *appreciation*?"

I thought about it, but nothing surfaced. "I don't know."

"Whether it's positive or negative, you should never give with the expectation that you'll get something in return. This is the foundation of manipulation."

"I don't want to manipulate anybody," I said, shaking my head.

"It's not your intent, but it is the manifestation nonetheless," he said. "Give with an open hand."

"Uh huh," I said, absentmindedly. My phone was lighting up every ten seconds. I couldn't take my mind off it.

Shah noticed my lack of interest and followed my gaze. "It's eating you up, isn't it?"

"No, no, I'm just—" I couldn't think of anything to say.

"Do you think it's important?"

"Probably not," I said, my eyes trying to sneak a peek.

"Then ignore it," he said. "Have you tried breathing exercises to calm yourself?"

"We did a meditation thing at work once, but it wasn't for me. I didn't get it."

"Didn't get what?"

"The feeling you're supposed to get," I said, rolling my eyes towards the ceiling. "I don't know, enlightenment?"

"Meditating isn't like filling up a tank of gas," he said. "It's a practice that takes years to master."

"I don't have *years* to master something new. My master's degree took long enough."

"Yet it didn't appear to teach you anything useful."

"Meditating isn't going to pay the bills, Shah."

"Perhaps not," he said. "But it will train your mind to eliminate distractions. Having the ability to reach deep focus may help you *pay the bills*, no?" He smiled gently as he waited for my reply.

"Maybe," I said, softening. "Okay, what do I do?" I snuck one last look at my phone, which was buzzing enough to almost fall off the table.

"First, close your eyes," he said. "Take a deep breath in…a deep breath out. Now, I want you to slow down your breaths."

"Like this?" I asked, as I attempted to breathe slowly.

"That's fine," he said. "Now, I want you to count your breaths and envision the breath inflating…then deflating, like a balloon."

I breathed until the count of twelve. "What do I do now," I said through one open eye.

"Continue."

"Until when?"

"Until I tell you to stop."

I continued to breathe. After some time, I felt hazy. Then a barrage of thoughts flew into my head. What did I need to finish tonight? I think I'm hungry. What was that song I heard earlier?

I started the count over, only making it to six before I started envisioning Frank laughing over an emptied glass of bourbon.

"How long?" I demanded.

"Until I tell you to stop."

"I can't do this," I said, opening my eyes. "I'm just not meant to meditate, I guess."

"We both know that's not true."

"What kind of skill is this anyway? Just sitting still and breathing?"

"No one said it was a skill," Shah said.

"But you're using it to get to enlightenment."

"I can think of quite a few people who would be offended by your simplification of meditation."

"Then what is it for?"

"It's not *for* anything," he said. "It's a process. Again, you're too hung up on the end result."

I huffed. "Okay, I'll try again."

I closed my eyes. This time I couldn't get to the count of five before I heard a buzz that caused my eyes to crack open. I thought maybe Shah didn't notice.

"Do you want to answer that phone?"

My eyes popped open. "Yes. I just want to see if it's Nikki, to make sure nothing is wrong."

Shah sat silently. I grabbed the phone and saw that I had thirty-nine unread text messages, all from Frank Benjamin. It began with "Are u around?" and ended with "Where the hell are u?" and "I need u."

"I need to make a call," I told Shah.

He looked at the clock, looking tired and suddenly twenty years older. "Our session is done for today anyway." I waved and ran out of his room, the phone already against my ear.

***

Back at the office, Frank was meeting with a balding man who looked terrified.

"Have a seat, Kumar," Frank said cheerily, as I entered his office. Apparently, he'd gotten over my absence. "This is the young hotshot I told you about, Danny."

Frank introduced the man as Daniel Toole, President of Evetrin, another company that was struggling of late. Frank caught me up to speed. "We were just discussing a plan to take over Evetrin."

"You mean a merger," Toole said, timidly.

"Yes, merger. Sorry," Frank said, not seeming too concerned. "Evetrin has hit some hard times and can use the help."

"We're excited to be part of the Green Point family," Toole said, not entirely convincing.

"What's my role in this exactly?" I asked.

"I'd like you to be the point man in creating a smooth transition for both teams," Frank said.

"Which would involve what?" I asked. This was all so sudden and confusing.

"You'll meet with our departments a few times a week," Toole said. "You will decide how our employees can serve you best."

"How many employees is that?" I asked.

Toole looked nervously toward Frank, who took over

the conversation. "This is what we've been discussing. We can't possibly take on *all* of Evetrin's employees due to health care, retirement, etc. We'll need to make some— *adjustments.*"

I noticed Toole looking down at the table. Adjustments were of course a euphemism for layoffs. He started to gather his things. "So unless there's anything else?" Toole said.

"No, I think we're good." Frank said. "Kumar?"

I nodded my head, even though I knew nothing about the deal.

Toole shook our hands and left the room. Frank could hardly contain his excitement. "This is big," he said.

"What is this about?" I asked. "Why are we merging with Evetrin?"

"It's what we talked about, Kumar; about adapting. This is our chance to capture an additional twenty percent of the market."

"But I thought we were branching out?"

He waved his hand, dismissing my words. "We can walk and chew gum at the same time, Kumar."

"But it sounds like we're going to cost them a lot of jobs."

"It's that or the company goes under and they *all* lose their jobs," Frank said. "Do you want to be responsible for *that*?"

"No, but I'm concerned that we're spreading ourselves too thin." I was suddenly feeling overwhelmed, just thinking about the extra work load this would add to my already packed schedule.

"Do you know the main goal of a corporation like ours?" Frank asked me.

"To build a strong brand and develop quality products."

"Oh Kumar, I thought you were brighter. It's the stock price. If the stock price rises, then I wouldn't care if we were selling dirt in a box."

"But don't we have *some* responsibility to the workers?"

"The workers have the option of working somewhere else."

"But they don't even get a warning. It just seems—selfish."

"The market is selfish, Kumar," he said. "That's why it works. We all chase self-interest and through that, all boats are lifted. Do you disagree?"

"I believe in a free market economy," I admitted. "But I think there's room for some compassion."

"You don't succeed with compassion. Compassion leads to falling behind in the marketplace. Will you have *compassion* when you're out of a job?"

"Couldn't we find another way to raise the share price?" I was desperately hoping Frank would see eye to eye with me.

"No," Frank said without a pause. "Taking over Evetrin is the best option right now. You choose what you do with the money we make. You can donate all you want. There's your compassion. Remember the gym I helped build?"

"You *gave the money* to build the gym," I pointed out. "You didn't help build it. And it bears your name."

"Because it wouldn't *exist* without me," he said, inching towards my face. "Why shouldn't my name be on it?"

I couldn't answer, feeling the heat of his sour breath.

"Save the hippie crap for your home life, Kumar," he said. "In business, it's kill or be killed. And I'm ready to kill."

"I can see that."

"Don't get smart, Kumar," he said. "You need this

more than I do."

The worse part was that he was right.

***

Frank instantly provided me with an expense account so I could update my wardrobe. I would be the main contact between Green Point and Evetrin and would have to meet with their representatives a few times per week until the merger was completed.

"How am I supposed to get my other work done if I'm dealing with Evetrin?" I asked Frank that morning.

"Have Cynthia help you," he answered as he rubbed a speck of dust off his desk.

"But that's not her position."

"It'll be good for her to learn some new skills," he said, nonchalantly. "I'm sure she won't mind."

Frank was correct about the last part. I asked Cynthia a few hours later if she would help me inspect the remaining prospectus, which had gotten nowhere since the Evetrin deal. I gave her instructions and created a score sheet so she would know what to look for.

"Sure," Cynthia beamed, "I can do that."

"Really? It's not a burden?"

"Not at all! I have some free time. Plus, it'll be good for me to learn what you guys do. Maybe I'll take over someday," she said with a wink.

"Okay, I'll be out in meetings with the Evetrin folks all day," I said. "You have my number if you need."

"I'm sure it'll be fine. Enjoy your day. You look good today, Kumar. I don't know what it is."

It was the suit. And I did look good. For the first time, I felt like a genuine power-broker. My Brooks Brothers attire delivered a sense of confidence that eight years of schooling couldn't accomplish.

I was ready to kill.

Chapter Twelve

"We cannot change anything until we accept it.
Condemnation does not liberate, it oppresses."
–Carl Jung

I decided to walk from the office to Shah's. I told myself it was to get some exercise, but I knew, deep down, that it was *really* to show off my executive wardrobe.

Before that day, I'd paid little attention to other's clothing. I wore bargain basement suits, whatever looked acceptable, for the lowest price was my constitution. But after the salesman showered my ego with praise, talking about how it shed years off my face, I saw the world differently. Fashion was all I could see. I sized up the other businessmen on the street, scoffing at their imitation watches, their thrift store-chic clothing. They seemed pathetic to me, like they didn't respect themselves enough to wear something stylish. I took pleasure in dressing down my fellow pedestrians.

Then I noticed a dark cloud emerge above me, as if it had been following me for the past few blocks. I was still several blocks from Shah's. A single, thick raindrop fell on the sidewalk in front of me. I looked up to see the cloud develop into a black mass, swallowing the sky around it. The cloud let go a downpour that accumulated within seconds. I jogged the rest of the way, but couldn't save myself from being doused from the rain. Only a block away from Shah's, a delivery truck cut by me, driving straight into a deep puddle. The water splashed over me like a personal tidal wave. I was soaked from head to toe.

I entered Shah's apartment looking like a drowned rat in my Brooks Brothers attire, which was sticking to me like a wet suit. Shah laughed as I sloshed into his room, my footsteps causing piercing squeaks on the old wood floor. He grabbed a towel from the bathroom, still laughing at me.

"I fail to see what's funny about this," I said, taking the towel and mopping up the drips of water on my face and neck.

"You look like a rag. What's not funny about that?"

"This is a $10,000 rag. Now it's probably ruined because an idiot trucker decided to be funny."

"You're much better off appreciating the comedy in times like these," he said, taking a seat. "Self-pity does no one any favors."

"I'm just supposed to forget it and laugh it off," I said, stewing with annoyance.

"Unless you plan on seeking revenge against nature, I hardly see any other option," he said.

"Why can't you just let me be angry?"

"You, of course, have the right to *choose* to be angry," he said. "I'm only saying that releasing the anger into a hearty laugh will keep you breathing a bit longer."

I could barely hear him over the chatter of my teeth. "Haha," I said sarcastically. "Can we move on?"

"As you wish," he said. "Let's begin with the phone call."

"What phone call?"

"Funny," he said. "It was the most important thing to you the last time we met. You mentioned your family calling you."

"What? No, it was Frank," I said, absentmindedly. "He wanted to know where I was."

"And where were you?"

"Huh? I was here."

"Really?" he said, his voice rising. "Because you didn't seem very present. That phone was controlling you. Then you used your family as an excuse. Would I be wrong in assuming that you knew it would be Frank?"

I looked at the floor. "The thought crossed my mind."

"Are you at his beck and call?"

I looked up. "No, I *chose* to take that call. I could have continued meditating, but it wasn't working. So, I took the call."

Shah sighed. "Fair enough," he said wearily. "Why did Frank desire your presence so badly?"

"He was working out a deal for a merger with another agency that—never mind. It's complicated and you probably wouldn't understand."

Shah smiled. "Probably not, but go on."

"He needed me to sit in on the meeting."

"Did he?"

"Well—he *said* he needed me. I didn't really do much. I'm not crazy about the guy, honestly."

"About Frank?" he asked, raising his eyebrows.

"No, no, no," I shook my head and continued, "With Daniel Toole. He's the guy we were meeting."

"You do, however, seem quite enthralled with Frank," Shah said.

"Sure," I said. "He's powerful, vibrant, good-natured. He looks and acts twenty years younger than he is."

"And these are the qualities you aspire to?"

"If I could be fifty percent of what Frank is, I'd be satisfied. I mean, everybody has to have a mentor, right?"

"Aah," Shah said, nodding. "One of the first sensible things you've said in a while." I smiled at his remark.

He continued. "Misguided, but sensible." My smile disappeared. "Now why were you summoned to the meeting?" he asked.

"I'm going to be the point man in closing the merger between their company and Green Point."

"*Point man*," he repeated. "These funny phrases. How will you manage?"

"I always manage," I said confidently.

"You didn't appear to be managing very well last week."

"That's before I recruited an assistant," I said proudly.

"Oh?" he said, raising an eyebrow.

"Yeah, I asked a colleague to…assist me with the day-to-day stuff. It opened up my day so I can work with Eve… the other company."

"So you're dumping your work on someone else?"

"I'm not *dumping* work on her. She's happy to do it. That's what she said anyway."

"I'm sure she's thrilled," Shah said. "Does she understand the amount of work she's taking on? Have you trained her on any of it?"

"Of course, or else she wouldn't have accepted."

"Or she could have accepted because she holds goodwill toward you," he said.

I ignored his statement. "Besides, it'll be good for her to learn new skills. She can be a larger value for the company."

"She provides more value because she lets others take

advantage of her?"

"I'm not—," I sighed, trying to compose myself. "She's helping me."

"It sounds like you're helping yourself to avoid the challenges of your job."

"But you—," I was losing my patience with what I construed as Shah's contradictory advice. "I'm trying not to burn myself out here."

"Then perhaps you shouldn't have taken the position if you weren't ready to *embrace* the challenges that came with it."

I smirked. "It almost seems like you don't want me to have this job. What's your agenda?"

Shah laughed. "Wolves have agendas," he said. "I'm simply a curious old man."

"No, this is getting me thinking," I said, leaning in. "Why am I coming here? What's your connection to Green Point?"

"Would it change anything if you knew?"

"Probably not, but I'm a curious young man."

"We're a bit late in the game for you to become curious."

"You're right," I said. "I should have vetted you from the beginning. I was a fool to just agree to see you."

"Why *did* you come to see me then?"

"Because the Board of Directors insisted upon it, Frank told me."

"Do you think the board or Frank would set you up with someone who had an *agenda*?"

"I supposed not."

Shah relaxed. "Paranoid men will find a conspiracy everywhere they look. As humans, we crave cause and effect to make sense of our world. It's too difficult for the logical thinker to accept that things just *are*."

"Just *are* what?" I asked.

"Just *are*. Things happen because they happen. Chaos reigns."

"How uplifting," I said, sarcastically.

"I don't mean to sound pessimistic," he said, chuckling. "It's how you deal with this chaos that matters, not what you *do*. When you came in today, soaking wet, how did you feel?"

"Cold and wet."

"And?" he asked, gesturing with his hand for me to elaborate.

"Mad."

"Exactly," he said. "There was nothing you could do about the rain, or the fact that water is wet, or that your suit doesn't respond well to lots of water. But you could do something about your reaction to getting wet. You chose to be angry, which flooded your mind with negativity toward the truck driver, to yourself, to the universe. You could have chosen to enjoy feeling wet, to dance in the rain, to laugh at how ridiculous you looked. You would have felt better and had a good story to tell."

"So you're saying it doesn't matter what I do because I'm screwed either way?"

He shook his head. "If you want to take it that way. But that's an awfully negative way to look at it."

"You planted the seeds." I pointed my finger at him, accusingly.

"Speaking of which, thank you for planting those seeds. Someday soon we'll enjoy a sweet lemon together so you can see the fruits of your labor."

"Can't wait," I said sarcastically.

"Did you plant those trees?" he questioned me.

"Of course I did."

"Why didn't you hire someone else to do it?" he asked. "That seems to be the way you operate."

"Because—," I paused to think. "I hadn't really thought of it honestly. Because it was a challenge, I guess."

Shah's eyes lit up. "Ahh, so you embraced the challenge even though it was out of your realm of expertise? Interesting."

I rolled my eyes. "Okay, I see where you're going with this."

"How did you feel after digging through the dirt, planting the seeds?"

"It felt good," I said, hating to admit this to him. "I felt like I earned it."

"Earned what?"

"The feeling of accomplishment."

"What drove you to completion?"

"Nothing really," I said. "I don't remember thinking about anything really. I just…did it."

"It happened because it happened."

"There you go again," I said.

"Embrace challenges, Kumar; like you did with the trees. But embrace the *right* challenges."

"How will I know which are the *right* challenges?"

"The same reason you know you married the *right* person. The same way you decide the *right* behavior for your children to display. Listen to your instinct. Be mindful of your emotional state. It is your compass."

"But every time I think I'm doing the right thing, I come back in here and you tell me that I'm wrong."

"Because you're not listening to your instinct. You're listening to Frank, to society; for them to tell you how to behave when you *know* that it's not right for you."

"You're quite presumptuous, you know. How do you know what I think?"

"Because you continue to return to me."

Chapter Thirteen

"Always do right – this will gratify some and astonish the rest."
—Mark Twain

Cynthia seemed eager to get started on the week's work, greeting me as I walked into the office that morning. She expressed confidence in being able to analyze my reports, along with other daily minutia to be handled. Remembering what Shah said, I considered withdrawing my proposal to Cynthia. But the morning rush washed away any doubts. Plus, she seemed in such a cheery mood that I felt I would be restraining her positive attitude if I took away her new privileges.

That Tuesday, Frank and I were to meet with Evetrin's human resources department to discuss potential downsizing, which would occur after the merger went through. Frank wasn't happy at having to be dragged in to see these people.

"It's a dog and pony show," Frank muttered as we walked into Evetrin's headquarters. "These guys will try to dazzle us with numbers we don't understand, hoping we'll smile and nod like numbskull teenagers."

"If you have such problems with them, why are you looking to merge?"

"It's not Evetrin that I have a problem with. I have problems with everybody. You need to look at these things like the modern-day version of a gladiator matchup. It's us against them; the loser is fed to the lions."

"But we're looking to join up. What is our objective

exactly?" I asked, speeding up my gait to match Frank's. For an old guy, he still had a spark in his step, like he was perpetually going to war.

He looked back at me as he talked quietly. "We're merging, sure, but that doesn't mean our two companies are split down the middle. I need to make it clear that Green Point is *absorbing* Evetrin, not the other way around. They want to keep employees on the payroll so they can have a more equal presence. Not going to happen."

"It sounds like they're just trying to protect jobs," I reasoned. "Shouldn't we work *with* them?"

"In business, you're never working *with* anybody," he sneered. "Everybody is on the lookout. When you least expect it, none of these guys will hesitate to tear out your throat."

"Yikes."

"What you have to do is one-up the other guy. We have approximately three minutes to assert dominance in that room or we're toast."

"How do I do that?"

"*You* don't need to do anything but keep quiet on this one," he said. "You'll see how it's done. The silent partner is always more menacing anyway."

Of all the adjectives used to describe me, menacing wasn't in the top hundred.

Tom Turner and Emily Vissotti sat on opposite ends of the boardroom desk. A power move, I immediately understood. Just as Frank predicted. The two HR goons were sandwiching us so that we would be surrounded, a psychological tactic to make us doubt that we were in control of the conversation.

I tried to think of a countermove, desperately wanting

to impress Frank. "I'm sorry," I said after we exchanged pleasantries. "I'm feeling a bit under the weather. Do you mind if I sit closest to the door in case of—you know."

Tom, who sat nearest the door, laughed and looked at Emily. They shared a moment of nonverbal communication, understated gestures that looked like a secretive, intense game of charades. I could feel Frank's grin as Tom stood up.

"Sure," he said, eliciting a fake smile. "No problem."

Tom lumbered to the other side of the table and sat next to Emily, whose frown told the real story. Frank gingerly took a seat next to me. We had just pulled off the boardroom equivalent of taking their queen.

After a mind-numbing ten-minute introduction, Emily moved onto the primary focus of our discussion. "Let me address the elephant in the room," Emily said. "And no, I'm not talking about Tom." Only Tom laughed. Emily cleared her throat. "We're to understand that there will be a certain number of layoffs made within the companies following the merger's completion."

"Within the *company*," Frank corrected her. "We're one big happy family, remember?"

Emily laughed bitterly. "Not quite yet," she said. "We need to come to an understanding that is…equitable for both parties before we can start this…big, happy family." Frank grunted in response. Emily continued. "To have a happy family, you need to have happy employees. Evetrin has always maintained that we have a responsibility to our employees and their families—"

"What about your responsibility to your shareholders?" Frank spat.

"Just give me a minute, Frank, and let me explain. We

live in a rapidly changing world. People are understandably on edge, afraid their jobs might disappear any minute—"

"They should be afraid," Frank said. "If they're not useful in a changing world, then they get left behind. That's simple economics."

"That's true," Tom said, standing up. Emily seemed to be getting annoyed at Frank's constant interruptions. "According to the market, one has to adjust. But, unfortunately as a business, we deal with people. People are more complicated, more emotional, than a statistical model."

"That's the problem," Frank said. "We get bogged down in emotional decision making. Pretty soon we're making concessions on anything the workers want. This is how the unions got out of control."

"We don't feel that simply wanting job security is asking for too much," Tom said. "A lot of money is involved in this deal and we feel that it's a tad unfair to be profiting in this way while employees are let go."

"Oh you think it's unfair?" Frank said, faking sympathy. "Well let's give everyone a *car* too, would that make things *fair*? Or how about they all get to be CEO? I can step down."

"Frank, please," Emily said, rubbing her head. He was defeating her spirits.

"We're going to need to take this seriously if we're going to make a deal," Tom said. "These are people's *lives* we're talking about."

"That's correct, it is people's lives, which includes my life, your life, Kumar's life," he said, pointing to me. I smiled awkwardly. "Why are our interests ignored? Why do we worry about our employees' well-being, but ignore our own?"

"Well to be fair, Frank, you do quite well, financially," Tom said, trying to remain civil.

"Yes, I do quite well because I've been smart and don't concern myself with being *unfair* to my employees," he said. "They understand that they have to be smart and adaptable in order to succeed. If they don't adapt, they're gone. If you clearly outline that vision, people understand and work with it. You can't fall back on this *fairness, everybody-gets-a-trophy* crap. That's how *your* situation happened."

"Oh and what situation is that?" Emily said, now alert and clearly frazzled by Frank's putdown.

"I'm not here today because I think it's fun to take over other companies," Frank said.

"Could have fooled me," Emily said out of the corner of her mouth. Tom held out a hand to calm her down.

"Frank, let me remind you that it's a *merger*, not a takeover," Tom said.

"Sure, whatever helps you sleep at night," Frank said. "But we're discussing this *merger* today because Evetrin was struggling. Am I correct?"

Tom and Emily nodded reluctantly.

"Your CEO, Daniel Toole, came to me, *pleading*, for help. If I didn't come to your rescue, *all* of your employees could lose their jobs. Am I also correct here?"

They nodded again.

"We deal in the same business." Frank said, his voice now smooth and velvety as he went for the kill. "My company is number one in the industry and yours…isn't in the top five. Why is this, do you think?"

"Get to the point Frank," Emily said, looking down at the table.

"Here's my opinion on why," Frank said. "It's not because of me, if that's what you're expecting. At least not *completely* because of me. Our success comes from having good workers. I ensure we have good, focused, *adaptable* workers by being clear about my expectations. No emotions are involved, just solid rule of law. They know what I want and they do what I want. Get it?"

"Yes, I think we understand," Tom said. "Can we please move on?"

"Not quite yet. You had your ten minutes," Frank said. "You need to take responsibility for your place in the industry. It might be difficult to hear but you're not as good as Green Point. Sorry, you're not. The market proves this. Now I'm willing to take a chance and absorb Evetrin, continue your employee health plans, and change as little as possible. But I can't do this if you're not willing to capitulate something."

"But we *are* capitulating, Frank," Tom said, relieved that he was finally able to speak. "We've offered to lay off a *fourth* of our workforce once the merger goes into effect."

"One-fourth would be how many workers?" Frank asked.

"Approximately 2,000," Tom said.

"There you go," Frank said. You have a smaller workforce than us and one-fourth doesn't constitute that many people. I could get 2,000 people together next week for a party if you needed. That wouldn't reduce our burden of taking on Evetrin."

"But you gain skills, creativity, from our workers," Emily insisted. "We're not trading crop futures. Humans have potential that you can't put a monetary value on."

"Oh, can't you?" Frank said. "So are we to understand

that all humans are equal in regards to intelligence and ability?"

"No, probably not," Emily said.

"If that's true, then how can we justify treating all of our employees the same?" Frank said. "Especially when we objectively know that my employees possess more skills than yours. I want at least 6,000 job cuts if we're going to take this conversation seriously."

"*Six-thousand?*" Tom said incredulously. "That's *three-quarters* of our entire staff!"

"Exactly," Frank said. "And you get to keep the strongest fourth of your workforce. You'll come out of this a much stronger company. Or *we* will come out of this a much stronger company."

"Frank, this is more complicated than—"

"Oh it's never more complicated," Frank interrupted. He now owned the room. "We only make it that way. We create chaos. You are creating chaos by letting your employees bully you. Do you know what happens when we give in to bullies?"

Tom shook his head and sighed.

"The bully destroys you," Frank said. "The bully now knows your vulnerability."

"I'm afraid I'm lost in your metaphor," Tom said. Beside him, Emily looked ready for a stiff drink.

"What's to keep your workers from demanding more when you give in? Next, it's executive-level health plans, preferred stock options, equity sharing," Frank said, taking a dramatic pause to let his final question sink in. "Where does it end?"

"Frank, I think you're being a bit dramatic," Tom said.

"Oh, am I?" Frank said. "I've been doing this stuff

since you two were watching Saturday morning cartoons. Do you doubt that I know how the marketplace works?"

"Of course not, Frank," Tom said. "We're simply conveying the information passed down from corporate. And they tell us that cutting 2,000 jobs is enough to satisfy the merger's conditions."

Frank slammed the table in exaggerated cheer, making everyone at the table, myself included, jump to attention. "Great then," he said. "Now you can march right back into corporate and tell them that I want 6,000 cuts."

"What about 4,000?" Tom bargained.

Frank weighed the option, shrugging his shoulders. "I'll consider it, but any less than that and I'm not answering the phone. Neither will Kumar. Right, Kumar?"

I wasn't sure if I was supposed to answer, but then saw Frank's hot gaze. "Yeah," I said wearily.

Tom shifted uncomfortably in his seat. "I'll talk to management."

Frank jumped out of his seat. I followed his lead. "It's been a pleasure chatting with you both," he said, flashing that trademark grin.

***

I was silent on the ride back to the office. Frank took this as an opportunity to recount the lessons learned from our meeting. "Did you see how I manhandled them?" he said, clearly proud of his show of power. I nodded silently.

He continued. "You can't let others walk all over you in business," he said. "You choose to either be predator or prey. I don't know about you, but I'll choose predator every time."

Frank looked over at me, noticing my silence. "You okay over there?" he asked.

"Yeah," I whispered. "It's just—" I trailed off.

"Out with it," he demanded. "Honesty, remember?"

"It just doesn't seem right that we're going to cause so many to lose their jobs."

"*Right* is relative," Frank said. "We have this idea that right and wrong are set in stone, but that's not reality. What's right for me might not be right for you, and vice versa."

"But we're causing pain for these people and their families."

"You've been talking with yogi freak too much," he said. "Pain is necessary. Pain is good. Sure, some people will lose their jobs—"

"Four-thousand people," I interrupted.

"Well, let's hope more than that," he cackled. "Anyway, they'll learn new skills and get a job somewhere else. This may end up being the biggest blessing of their lives."

"I doubt it," I whispered.

"You'll see," he said. "I've been in this game a lot longer than you have."

Frank left me with those words as he dropped me off outside the office. He peeled away, waving as his Aston Martin faded from view.

I decided to check in and see how the day went for Cynthia. But when I entered the office, I almost choked.

Dave sat at my desk, his head deep in a pile of scrambled papers. He didn't even notice me walk in. "Dave?" I said, knocking on the door.

He looked up with a smile. "Oh, hey, Kumar. Was just finishing up this batch here."

"What are you doing?" I asked. I couldn't contain my dissatisfaction at seeing Dave behind my desk.

"I'm evaluating these prospectus," he said. "Sorry, I thought you knew. Cynthia got crushed and needed some help."

"Is that so?" I said. Dave now looked worried based on my reaction. "Excuse me a moment," I said.

I stormed out to Cynthia's desk, but found it empty. An intern sat nearby organizing files. "Hi, umm, Kathy?" I said, approaching the intern.

"Jamie," she corrected.

"Yeah, do you know where Cynthia is?"

"She had a family emergency and had to leave," Jamie said.

"Is that so?" I said, already walking away.

I grabbed my cell and walked into an empty conference room. It was bad protocol to call Cynthia at home in the middle of a crisis, but I couldn't help it. The image of Dave sitting at my desk tore me up inside.

The phone rang three times before Cynthia's tiny voice answered. "Kumar?" she said.

"Yeah, it's me," I said. "Sorry to bother you. Everything okay?"

"Oh yeah, thanks for checking in," she said, misinterpreting the call. "My idiot ex couldn't pick up Ryan at school so I had to get him. Do you need me to come back?"

"Well, it's too late now," I spat.

"Is everything okay?" she asked, sensing the edge in my voice.

"No, not exactly," I said.

"I figured you and Dave are friends and he's a smart guy—"

I scoffed at her statement, interrupting her.

"Was that bad?" she asked innocently.

"Well, yeah," I said. "Those documents were supposed to be private."

"But—you let me work on them," she said.

"Yes, I *entrusted* them to you. Now Dave has seen them. Did you give them to anyone else? Maybe Patti from accounting? Gene in sales?"

"No, Kumar!" she protested, a tinge of annoyance in her tone. "Just Dave. I thought you and him—"

"You should never *assume* in business," I said. I could hear her choking back tears on the other end. "Let's talk about this tomorrow. Have a good night."

"You too," said through her tears.

Now it was time to deal with Dave. I marched back into my office, where Dave continued to slump over the documents. "I'm going to need you to stop working on those," I said.

Dave stretched. "Thank God," he said. "My head is killing me. I don't know how you do this all day long."

"I don't do this all day," I said. "Cynthia was supposed to do it."

Dave shrugged, unaware of my annoyance. "Do you need me to do anything else?"

That's when a thought crept into my brain. Dave was trying to learn my methods so he could take my spot. I knew Frank wouldn't think twice to can me if I screwed up the merger. Maybe Frank had *already* planned to replace me. Maybe Dave was in on it.

"Why?" I asked, narrowing my eyes in accusation.

Dave looked confused. "To help you out. Cynthia said you were stressed with the new job."

"I'm doing just fine," I grumbled.

"Okay then," he said, gathering his things. "Now that I've seen it, I got to ask you about this assignment."

"What about it?"

"What's it about?" he asked. "All these random investments. Are we transitioning into something else?"

"No."

"Okay, but you would tell me if we were, right? Because it doesn't make sense that we would be merging anytime soon. I just want to know if my job is threatened, that's all."

"I'm not at privilege to tell you," I said, avoiding eye contact.

"You're not at *privilege*? Kumar, you sound like the HR department. We can talk to each other like friends."

"You really shouldn't have seen those," I said, pointing to the documents. "That was supposed to be classified."

"But you gave them to Cynthia."

"I *entrusted* them to her. She broke my trust," I said, sitting down at my desk. This felt better.

Dave turned his head sideways, questioning. "What's up with you, Kumar?"

"Nothing," I said. "What do you mean?"

"You sound so different right now, the way you're speaking."

"Why were you so eager to go over these documents?"

"Because I wanted to help you," Dave said. "I assume you still know what that means, to *help*?"

"No one *helps* someone for no reason. You wanted something from this."

Dave stepped forward, challenging me. "What are you implying?"

"I know you were jealous that I got the VP slot," I said. "I could read it on your face. You hate that I'm in charge."

"I've never thought of you as *in charge,* to be honest. I just thought of you as a friend. But I guess that's not the case."

"There's no friends when it comes to business," I said. "There's only predator and prey."

Dave's raised his eyebrows. "You keep telling yourself that, whoever you are," he said. He started to walk out of the office, but turned around before reaching the door. "Do you know why I really wanted to help?"

I smirked. "Ahh, the truth will set you free."

"Because I admire you, Kumar," he said. "I admire your drive, your work ethic. I've always been kind of a slacker and wanted to be driven, like you. But now I see what happens when the drive takes over."

I held my smirk, not wanting Dave to think he'd affected me. "Are you done?" I asked.

"Yeah, I am done," he said, leaving without another word.

Chapter Fourteen

*"It's not the load that breaks you down,
it's the way you carry it."*
–Lou Holtz

The relationship between Cynthia and I soured from then on. We still communicated, but our words were clipped and impersonal. It was understood that she would continue to perform minor administrative tasks for me, but would no longer handle the analysis. Her initial offer to help now turned into a duty, for she feared what Frank would do if she obstructed my duties with the Evetrin merger.

"Mr. Vedig," she said to me the next morning. She now called me Mr. Vedig. "You had a message from Mr. Applen."

"Who?"

"That's all he said," she said dismissively. I noticed she avoided looking me in the eyes.

I felt a tinge of guilt, seeing her like this. I wanted to apologize about the previous night's phone call, but my need to not look weak overpowered this sensation. "Thank you for taking my call," was the best I could come up with.

"My pleasure," she spit, full of venom.

I returned the call to Mr. Applen. He answered as if he were waiting for my call. "Kumar," he said. "Great to hear from you."

"My head must not be on right, because your name isn't registering," I said, confused.

"It's not you," he said. "We haven't met. I'm John Applen and I work with Swift Technologies and I'm a good friend of Frank's."

"Oh okay. A friend of Frank's is a friend of mine."

"Of course," he said. "Frank mentioned that you were shopping for a club membership. I figured I can take you over to Palmwood on Saturday and introduce you to a few people."

I thought about Dave and the ending of our friendship. Maybe it was time to move up in the social world. "Sure," I replied.

***

Saturday came after a blistering two days of undoing Dave's mistakes with the prospectus. At that point, I held so much animosity toward him that I didn't feel a tad bit guilty for throwing away our friendship. John Applen greeted me outside the front entrance, wearing a white, collared shirt and shiny, spotless golf cleats. I had planned to park my car, but upon seeing Applen, I decided to have a valet park it.

We shook hands and Applen watched the valet drive off. "Be sure to inspect your car when you get it back. These guys, you know?"

I didn't know, but nodded in agreement anyway.

Applen introduced me to three of his friends, who already appeared tipsy from afternoon martinis. We hung out at the bar for another twenty minutes. The guys discussed rumored mergers, major market movers, and something they cryptically referred to as "The Project." I felt like a bystander, unable to think of anything to add.

"Is Frank coming today?" I asked Applen.

"Don't think so," he said, glancing around. "He usually

joins us on Saturday, but I guess he had something come up today."

Applen finished up his final sip and gestured for us to follow him to the carts.

Every conversation with this crew involved competition, whether the topic was watches or which private school their kids attended. I avoided the last one, insecure that my kids still attended their local public school. I noted that I would need to look into new schools for next year.

I enjoyed their competitive style, finding myself trying to one-up their boasts of under-the-radar investments that turned out to be highly lucrative. If nothing else, I knew investments and could keep pace with this type of discussion.

"We heard you're getting into private equity at Green Point," one of the guys named Ron said. He was the loudest of the bunch, prone to hurling his club in anger when the ball didn't go where he wanted it to.

"A little bit," I said as I teed off.

"Oh yeah?" Ron inquired. "What you got going on in the portfolio?"

I swung and slapped the ball dead center; an ace shot. I turned around. "A master never reveals his secrets." I noticed Applen shoot Ron a serious look.

My golf game was possessed that day; I was as focused as humanly possible. My one goal that day was to win and prove to these guys that I was a big leaguer. By the last hole, I was up by over 10 strokes.

"Don't worry," I said as I clobbered the ball on the final hole. "I'm just having a good day."

I joined the guys for drinks following the game. The sunset over the club veranda was picturesque, reminding me how good I had it.

"So seriously, what are you guys up to over there?" Applen asked after our second martini. My head was beginning to swim, which loosened up my lips a bit.

"I won't tell you the name, but we're acquiring a minority stake on another business."

"What are we talking here? Insurance? Manufacturing?"

"Can't tell," I said, enjoying being mysterious.

"You're just going to torture me, huh?" he said.

"That's business," I said, finishing my last sip before ordering another with a finger point. "What about you guys?"

"Oh, we're just a humble little fund," he said. "We're just scouting right now. Nothing major."

After three more drinks, I hobbled out to the parking lot to retrieve my car. My red 328i rolled up, almost hitting me. I jumped out of the way and was about to ream out the driver. Then the window rolled down, revealing Frank.

"Get in," he said. "You shouldn't drive anyway."

"How..." I couldn't even finish the sentence.

"I practically own this club kid," he said with a smile.

***

"How was your day?" Frank asked with a sinister tone.

"Not bad," I said, proudly. "I smoked them."

"Good man," Frank said, tapping the wheel. "Let me ask you. How did you meet those guys?"

"Weirdly enough, Applen called me at the office," I said. "Said he was friends with you."

"You know how I feel about business and friendship."

"So you don't know him?" I asked.

"Oh, I know him fine," he said. "It's the friend part I don't know about. Those guys are vultures."

"How so?"

"They're hanging out with you to see what information they can get."

"Frank, you're just being paranoid," I said, neglecting to mention their questions. "They're just looking for a good time."

"Did you tell them anything? Be honest."

"No," I said firmly. "They weren't interested anyway."

"Of course they were," he said. "They're just good at making it seem like they don't care."

"It must be exhausting to think like you, Frank."

"Not one bit," he said. "Do I look exhausted?" I shook my head. "My point of view frees me to do what I do best: Run a business. Friends complicate that."

"But you have to admit that there's some positives that come from having friends."

"Sure, they let you borrow money," he said with a grin. "But I don't need to borrow money. Friendships in business are emotional investments. If you stay away from emotional investments, you'll have a much smoother ride to success."

"So you avoid friendships because you don't want to feel emotion?"

"I never avoid anything," he said quietly. "I *choose* to not let myself be dragged into something that I don't need. Outside of business, sure, I have plenty of friends. But I won't allow myself to be touched when it comes to competitors. And neither should you."

I could feel him looking at me. "What?" I said.

"Is it true that Dave Henderson has been looking at our investment files?"

"That wasn't me," I protested like a child caught

cheating. "I put Cynthia in charge and she handed off the work to Dave."

Frank sighed. "That's why you've got to do it yourself Kumar. Collaboration is for the weak and overwhelmed. Do you still feel overwhelmed?"

I felt like I was being interrogated. "No sir. I thought Cynthia could be trusted—"

"I can't have people looking at those investments willy-nilly. I put trust in you for a reason."

"I didn't realize they were so secretive."

"Assume everything is secretive unless I say otherwise," Frank said.

"I'm sorry, Frank. I messed up."

"Did anyone else see them?"

"No," I said. "Just Cynthia and Dave."

"Okay, I'll have a talk with them tomorrow." Frank slowed and pulled up to the curb. He opened the door to exit. "Kumar?" he said before stepping out.

"Yeah?"

"Let's not mess up again, okay?"

"It won't happen again," I said, ashamed at my pleading tone.

Chapter Fifteen

"It's not the years in your life that count. It's the life in your years."

–Abraham Lincoln

It was well past 11 when I finally got home. The kids were long in bed; another night not seeing their father. Nikki met me at the door and forced me outside.

"Where were you?" she demanded.

"I was golfing."

"Until 11?"

"Frank took me out after—"

She looked up at the sky. "Frank always takes you out after. You go out on more dates with him than you have with me for the past ten years."

"I don't really have a choice," I said, trying not to yell.

"You always have a choice," she said. She looked deep into my eyes. "Are you seeing someone else?"

My voice rose. "Come on! Of course not."

"You reek like alcohol."

"Like I said, I went out with Frank and the guys. They drink. Get over it."

"Get *over* it?" she repeated. "I barely see my husband. My kids barely see their father. Because you're out with the boys."

"Look, someday I'll be in charge and—"

"And what then?" she said. "You'll be too busy for us then too. Did you know your son got *suspended* from school yesterday?"

"What?" No. I'll talk with him."

"He doesn't need you to yell at him whenever he does something wrong. He needs guidance. He needs a *father*."

"I'm giving him guidance by succeeding."

"You're teaching him to ignore family if it means earning more money. Do you think that's a good lesson?"

"That's really unfair," I said.

"Why is that unfair?"

I couldn't answer.

She continued. "You need to get this under control and come back to your family."

"My family doesn't even like me!" I yelled, losing control. "I feel like an alien here! The only place I'm respected is at work."

"How can we respect someone who's never around? It's like we don't *know* you anymore."

I looked at the ground. She had me. "Maui is coming up in a couple months," I said, referring to the trip I'd surprised them with a while back. "It'll give me some time to spend with you guys. Some time to think things over."

"What do you do until then?" she asked. The sadness in her eyes almost broke my heart.

"I don't know," is all I could say.

***

I was a zombie throughout the next day; the combined effects of a hangover mixed with guilt. Passing by the front desk, I noticed Jamie, the intern, again in Cynthia's usual spot.

"Did Cynthia leave again?" I asked her.

"Yeah," she replied, motioning towards the hallway.

"She ran out of here crying a few minutes ago."

"What happened?"

"I don't know. She got a phone call and then she just left. She's really emotional," she whispered. I backed away and headed for the elevators.

Speed-walking along the third floor, I made it to Dave's office. The door was slightly open, so I peeked in. His stuff covered the desk, but no one sat behind it. I ran back out and asked the third floor secretary if she'd seen Dave.

"No, he didn't come in today," she said.

"Did he call in?" I asked.

"Nope," she said. "We haven't heard anything. Is he okay?"

"I don't know," I answered, as I turned around and headed back towards the elevator.

***

Back in my office, I sat silently, unable to focus. After a few minutes, I noticed my phone blink, indicating a call. I picked up the receiver.

"Kumar?" Frank said on the other end.

"Yeah," I half-whispered.

"You don't sound so good."

"What is it, Frank?" I steadied my voice.

"You should sound happier, now that your problem has been taken care of," he said cryptically.

"What are you talking about?" I asked, nervously.

"Cynthia and Dave," he said. "I sent them packing. Good riddance, right?"

"Why did you do that?"

"They were a liability," he said, his voice annoyingly

cheerful. "You said yourself that they knowingly inspected classified documents."

"I didn't say—"

"They *knowingly* inspected classified documents," he reemphasized.

"Fire *me* Frank. Spare them." I shocked myself with these words.

"Fine, you're fired," he said.

I breathed heavily into the phone. Was this a good thing? Was I a hero? Would he hire me back?

Before I could resolve these questions, Frank cackled on the other end. "Quit being stupid, Kumar."

"You can't do that to people," I said, almost breaking into tears.

"Okay, hear my point of view, okay? Before you judge. Deal?"

"Okay," I replied.

"Cynthia took on a task that you asked of her. I told you to ask her, correct?"

"Yes."

"Good so far," Frank said. "She then decided that she couldn't handle the task. Rather than call you or I, she *chose* to include someone else, someone who had no business looking at what he saw. That's a *huge* problem from my perspective."

"It was a mistake," I said, trying to reason with him. "She wanted to please me."

"But it was a mistake that could, and still can, cost us dearly."

"I don't get why these investments are so secretive. Are they on the level?"

"Why would I share them with you if they weren't?"

"To make me an accomplice," I said, a bit fearful of my challenging tone.

"Okay, I'm going to selectively forget that you just accused me of a crime," he said. "We'll chock it up to emotional stress."

"Then tell me!"

"I will, if you let me talk," Frank said. His composure was driving me crazy. "Kumar, what's the most valuable thing in the world?"

I groaned. "This game again?"

"Just tell me. What?"

"I don't know. Money?" I offered.

"Good guess, but no."

"Love?" I guessed.

"No, but nothing wrong with love," he said.

"Respect."

"Ahh, anyone can get respect," he said. "People respected Mussolini, right? No. It's *information*, Kumar. Anything can be duplicated, now. The only thing unique in us is the information in our brains. It's why Facebook, Google and all the rest run the world. Because they hold the information."

"Get to the point, Frank."

"I would have hoped that you already understood the point," he said, sounding a bit annoyed. "Cynthia and Dave now have information that they weren't privy to. There's no guarantee what they'll do with that information."

"What would Cynthia care about it?"

"Probably nothing," he said. "But that's the problem. She doesn't realize how valuable that information is. Let's say she mentions it to her husband? Her husband tells his friend, who happens to be a day trader. He tips off his buddies, and so on."

"You're talking about insider trading," I said.

"I'm talking about what happens in the real world," Frank said. "My point is that the information is loose, benefitting everyone else when it's supposed to be benefitting *us*. We own that information."

"What good does firing her do?" I asked. "She still has the information. In fact, she's probably more likely to tell someone now."

"That's why we're going to make that information useless."

"How?" I asked.

"We're cancelling all scheduled investments. We'll start over," he said. "I wasn't feeling too confident about it anyway."

"Frank, I just spent the past six months of my life preparing these," I said, my voice cracking. "Not to mention the contacts, the meetings, the relationships."

"What did I say about relationships?"

"But we're so far along," I said, feeling more panicked. "What about Evetrin? And the staff downsizings?"

"It looks like maybe they'll keep their jobs after all," he said. "That should make you happy."

"Six months of work for nothing," I said, mostly to myself.

"The library of Alexandria was burned down in a day," he said. "The human history of knowledge gone in an instant. Sometimes that happens. We have to destroy in order to build."

"But I sacrificed everything."

"And it won't be for naught, Kumar. You learned something from this experience. At least I *hope* you did."

"Don't trust my co-workers."

"There you go," he said with jolly cheer. "Listen, we have to fail sometimes to move forward."

"And how do we move forward?"

Just then, Jamie timidly opened the door, carrying a shiny, white stack of new documents.

"If I can correctly assume," Frank said, "that must be your new batch."

"You've got to be kidding me," I said, looking with dread at the hefty pile of documents Jamie dumped on my desk.

"Another lesson is the importance of cleaning up your own mess," he said, now gravely serious. "I need those results scanned and sent over by midnight tonight."

I slammed my head on my desk and stayed that way for the better part of an hour.

***

Hours later, the full moon lit up the corners of my office. It was nearing midnight as I finished the last analysis. My brain burned, my hand cramped. I considered sleeping on the floor of the office, so exhausted that I could barely muster enough strength to stand.

It was then that I realized that I'd missed my meeting with Shah.

I imagined the old man sitting in his chair, watching the clock, fidgeting with every creak he heard outside his door. Whereas before, I didn't dare miss a meeting because I feared for my job, now I felt bad for Shah. I felt sometimes that I was this lonely man's only connection to the world.

And I'd let him down.

Finally able to get out of the office, I vowed that I

would stop by Shah's tomorrow, just to say hello. This job had finally killed my spirit and I needed Shah to save me.

My stomach rumbled on the ride home so I stopped off for something to eat. The only places open were the greasy fast food joints, so I chose whichever was the closest, neglecting to even notice the restaurant's name.

I sat in my car and ate in the parking lot, watching a homeless couple settle down for the night behind the drive-thru window. Halfway through the meal, I felt a tingle in my left arm. Ignoring it, I continued to eat. The thoughts floated around my head like mayflies, impossible to focus on one and equally impossible to make disappear.

That's when the pain hit me. My chest felt like someone was squeezing me with all their might. My entire body shook. I was able to get the driver's door opened and I collapsed to the ground, trying to yell but failing to produce any sound.

The last thing I remembered was an older man looking over me. His face was calm, perhaps even smiling as he told me it would be okay. I knew that scar on the left cheek, the lazy eye. I could swear that it was Shah, if it made any sense that he would be hanging out at a fast food restaurant after midnight.

Then, everything went black.

Chapter Sixteen

"Why should I fear death?
If I am, death is not. If death is, I am not.
Why should I fear that which cannot exist when I do?"
—*Epicurus*

I woke up surrounded by blinding, white light. A constant beep was the only sound. My eyes adjusted to the light and I realized that I was lying in a hospital bed, covered in wires. An IV was hooked into my arm, which looked wrinkled and malnourished.

I tried to stand up but weakness and gravity pulled me back down. Nikki entered the room and saw that I was awake. She rushed over to me.

"Oh my God, you're awake!" she shouted. "How do you feel?"

"Like I was hit by a truck," I said. My voice sounded strange, alien, affected by days of cotton mouth. "What happened?"

"Honey, you had a heart attack."

I smiled weakly. "They almost killed me."

Nikki sighed and shook her head. "I knew this would happen."

"Did you talk to Frank or anybody from my work?"

"I called the next day and told them what happened."

"Who's going to finish the investments?"

"I don't think you need to worry about that right now," she said, holding my hand.

I tried to get up again, but Nikki held me down. "Look,

this was a gift. You could be dead right now. Your children could be without a father. You were given a second chance. You have to choose right now—your life or your job.

I licked my lips, feeling the dry skin crack. "You're right," I said.

She smiled. "That's what I like to hear," she said. "The kids are on their way. They'll be happy to see you."

"Will they?"

"Of course," she said, somewhat unconvincingly. "Let's forget the past and start over. This is your new life."

I looked around. "Not such a glamorous life so far." I noticed a card on the bedside table. "What's that?" I asked.

Nikki grabbed the card and handed it to me. "Oh, a man came by and dropped this off. He said he was a friend. He didn't give me his name, but he was so nice."

I opened the card; inside was a small page of notebook paper. On it was written:

You've been given the most important gift you can ever receive: Life. Don't screw up your second chance. I'll be waiting for you when you're ready. -Shah

"Who was he?" Nikki asked.

"An old friend." I replied, smiling.

***

I hadn't realized how out of control my life had become until I was forced to slow down. The next few weeks of recovery were painful and slow, but also wonderful. I found myself noticing the things around me, appreciating simple moments that I'd taken for granted. With no goal besides feeling better, I grew to enjoy being around my family; the way the kids lost their minds in the yard, the funny way that Nikki talked to them. They even let me in on their inside jokes.

I was relearning how to use my body, but also relearning how to communicate with the people who loved me. I took pleasure in the minor improvements. Raising my arm an additional inch or two was like winning the lottery. The pain became a challenge to overcome. I started taking short walks that turned into longer walks. The pain was always there, but I repudiated it with each step. I was winning.

But after a month or so, the honeymoon was over. As my body improved, I grew bored of the slow-paced lifestyle. Inwardly, I would wonder how Nikki and the kids could just sit around and enjoy themselves without accomplishing much of anything.

That's when the emails began.

It started innocently enough. I knew that my work email had piled up while I was out of commission. My doctor advised against checking it until I fully recovered, so as not to invite additional stress. "There's not much you can do about it now anyway," was how the doctor put it.

But I was feeling confident, and bored enough to delve into the emails. I received weekly updates from Frank; mostly financial information, updates to staff policy, nothing groundbreaking. That is, until I reached a couple weeks back and found this bombshell from Frank:

Hi Kumar,

Hope your recovery is going okay. I considered waiting to tell you, but I figured you should know, for preparedness sake. I've decided to rehire Dave Henderson, effective immediately. In your absence, it proved unsustainable to continue our outside investments. I considered shelving the project, but my better senses took over. Timing is of critical importance and if we are to be an industry leader, then we need to proceed. Since you took Dave under your wing and taught him your process, I feel that he's the only one right now who's capable of carrying out these tasks. At least when you return, Dave will serve as interim VP. But rest assured, your seat is only being kept warm until you recover.

Rest well my friend. —Frank

I read the email over four times until the subtext was clear. Dave had replaced me, pure and simple. In this world, interim led to permanent.

Ironically, I had set up my own fate by enabling Dave to learn my methods, even if the effect was unintended. Frank even used the phrase *took him under your wing* to suggest that I was grooming Dave to take over. What rubbish.

I then noticed an email from Dave, echoing Frank's decision and thanking me for getting him back, even though I had nothing to do with it. This needed to end immediately. I fired off an email to Frank, telling him that I'd recovered enough to work remotely until the end of the month, when I'd be able to return. These deadlines weren't approved by my doctor, but I'd worry about that later. I neglected to respond to Dave, figuring he'd learn soon enough that I was back.

Within a half hour, Frank responded back:

You're a true warrior! I knew you'd be back on your feet in no time. You have the heart of a tiger. That's what is going to drive you to the top. Attached are ten new investments opps. Please don't show them to anyone. I'll let Dave know that you're back. —Frank

As nice as it felt to be back in charge, at least electronically, I was happier to get Dave out of the picture. But I knew that, for now, I'd need to keep this secret, as Nikki would never have allowed me to work while I was still weak. I was aware that if I stayed away any longer, Dave would be sitting in my seat come next month. I couldn't have that.

To cover myself, I told Nikki that I was reading alone in the room. I made up a story of how the kids caused too much noise, which overwhelmed my fragile body. She fell for it without any hint of skepticism. I was able to spend the rest of the afternoon "reading" in peace, without a single distraction.

The next day, I decided to return to Shah's. Nikki was working and the kids were at school, so I didn't need to continue my secret spy game.

Shah's smile lit up the room when I entered. He rose out of his seat with an extended grunt and gave me a firm hug. "Glad to see you're still here," he said.

"Me too," I said, taking my old spot on the couch. "What a weird, scary experience to have to go through."

He sat back down. There were no animals around, it appeared. "Ahh, but we need these scary experiences to remind us that we're alive."

"I know that's true," I said, shaking my head. "I've really been able to look at my life in a new light."

"Good!" he exclaimed. "And what light would that be?"

"It's something Nikki said, that the kids almost had to grow up without a father. I'd been trying so hard to create a good life for them that I almost ruined their lives."

"Funny how that works, isn't it?" Shah said. Despite

his cheerful demeanor, he looked older, more frail. His breathing appeared more labored, as if I'd transferred my sickness to him. "Often, we don't realize what we have until it's gone," he said. "But you were fortunate enough to be given another chance."

"And that's the craziest part, how close I came to death," I said. "Being my age, I never put any thought that I could potentially not be around tomorrow."

"Does it bother you?"

"A little, yeah," I said. I thought it over. "Well, it bothers me a lot, actually."

"Why?"

"Why? Because death is scary. Non-existence is scary."

"Do you know what happens after you die?" he asked me.

"No, I don't," I said, not liking this type of questioning. "And I really hope you're not going to use my situation to prognosticate."

Shah laughed. "I'm not a prognosticator. I wouldn't even know how to spell it."

"So what happens when we die?" I asked, waiting for his philosophy.

"How would I know?" Shah said with a shrug.

"I thought you would have something profound to say about the afterlife."

"If I did, that would mean I'd either died or I'm making a blind assumption," he said. "I try not to make assumptions. And I'm pretty sure I'm still alive."

"Well, that's not comforting," I said.

"Why wouldn't that be comforting? It's the biggest mystery that links us all," Shah said. "We all die and no one knows what happens, no matter how much information we can cram into our brains. Isn't that nice?"

"I would use a different adjective rather than *nice*."

"Do you not like mystery? Surprise?"

"Call me silly, but I prefer to know things over not knowing."

"Because you're used to being in control," he said. "Death is the one thing we can't control, no matter how disciplined we may be. That can be frustrating to some."

"Okay, I get it," I said, settling to my default sour mood. "We're all going to die. Another uplifting message. I almost forgot how dreary your life lessons can get."

"Dreary? Accepting death is the ultimate path to freedom," he said. "If you're not afraid of death, then how can anything else scare you?"

"Well then, I guess I'm not free yet," I said, suddenly feeling uncomfortable. "Let's change the subject, shall we?"

"If you insist," he said. "How are you recuperating? You appear to be in somewhat good health."

"Yeah, I feel good," I said. "All that time taking things slow helped me out. I've even been able to get some work done."

"You're back already?"

"Sort of, yeah," I said. "I've been working from home. I've been able to get a lot done, surprisingly."

"What does your wife think of this?"

"She—" I paused, considered lying, but thought better of it, as Shah could always see right through me. "She doesn't exactly know yet. But I'll tell her."

"Because you're not supposed to be working?"

"Yeah, I guess," I said. "At least according to the doctor. But I feel just fine."

"Why did you feel the need to go back to work?"

I chose to leave the Dave situation out. "It just got so boring. I needed to do something."

"Do you find your family boring?"

"No, I didn't say that," I said.

"Is spending quality time with them not *doing something?*"

"No, I enjoyed the time with them," I said. "But when no one's around, I'm just alone with my thoughts."

"Thoughts of what?"

"Of death, I guess."

"Just what I thought," Shah said. "You disappear in your work because you fear death. Do you see how this irrational fear can impact your life?"

"So I'm just supposed to sit around and think about death all day?"

"No, you should *accept* death so you can stop troubling yourself over it," he said. "The more you worry, the more you risk another heart attack. You, worrying about death, may hasten your actual death."

"How's that for irony?"

"Have you tried the breathing exercises at all since we last tried?"

"Oh, this again," I said, rolling my eyes. "Remember when we tried last time?"

"But you were in a different place last time," he said. "You've seen how slowing down your life positively impacted you."

"Yeah, but it bored me."

"If you can meditate, you will never be bored again. Your brain is your worst enemy right now, with all these wandering, negative thoughts. Meditation helps you take charge of your mind. It will help you become more mindful and less distracted, less fixated on death and other trivialities."

I sighed dramatically. "Okay, let's do it."

"Remember that this isn't about *getting something*. The idea is to rid your mind of those fluttering thoughts. This is what causes you the anxiety that you feel."

"And how do I do this?"

"By focusing on your breathing. When you notice a stray thought, you need to return to your breath."

"And how will I know if I'm meditating?"

"You'll know."

On I went, back to the breath exercises. But this time, I lacked any of the irritation from our last session. I hadn't seen Frank in over a month so he no longer appeared as a phantom in my mind. In fact, I had almost forgotten what he looked like.

I did as Shah said, focusing on my breathing. At first, the thoughts bounced around like pin balls. But I kept returning to my breath every time a thought crept in. I'm not sure how much time elapsed, but the next thing I knew, I heard Shah's voice speaking to me.

"Kumar, are you there?"

I opened my eyes in panic, expecting to see the inside of a hospital. Instead, Shah smiled. "How do you feel?" he asked me.

I stretched. "Great actually. Did I fall asleep?"

"No," he said, still smiling. "You were sitting up the whole time."

"But how?" I don't remember anything."

"Exactly," he said, nodding. "You were meditating. There is nothing to remember."

I looked up at the clock. An hour had passed.

Chapter Seventeen

"Trust is the glue of life. It's the most essential ingredient in effective communication. It's the foundational principle that holds all relationships."
—Stephen R. Covey

Shah's words ran through my head the following day. Perhaps I was afraid of death, like he said. I needed to stop letting fear dictate my life.

These thoughts motivated me to return to work as quickly as possible. I figured that if I could prove to my doctor that I was healthy, he would sign off for my full return. This meant that I had to push even harder to deliver results.

I hunkered down in my secret office the next morning, confident that I wouldn't be disturbed. Nikki had a doctor's appointment so she would be gone most of the morning.

The Evetrin merger had gone through while I was away, with Dave taking charge in the negotiations. I made sure to assert myself in the project by making a call to Daniel Toole to announce my return. We had a nice chat, mostly formalities and promises to meet up in a few weeks when I was back on my feet.

But in the middle of the conversation, I heard the front door close. I quickly ended the call and quickly cleared my desk of any evidence of my work. Nikki walked in just as I shoved a ream of incriminating documents into my desk.

I swung around nervously. "Honey, what are you doing home?"

Her face was serious, flushed white. "They moved my appointment up," she said. "What were you doing?"

I immediately began to sweat and I fidgeted, trying to find an alibi. "I...uh...was reading."

"What were you reading?"

I looked at my now-empty desk. "Oh, I just put the book away because I was going to have some lunch. Do you want to order—"

She interrupted my pathetic excuse of an alibi. "Where were you yesterday?"

I froze. "When?"

"During the day," she said, moving closer. "I stopped over here on my break to see if you needed anything. You weren't here."

"I went for a walk."

"Where?" she questioned, looking me intensely.

I felt okay about telling the truth. "Remember that old man who came to the hospital room? I went to his house."

"Why didn't you tell me?"

"Oh, I didn't think it was important," I said, trying to sound casual.

"You've been *really* sneaky lately."

"No I *haven't*," I said, sounding childish.

"Are you seeing someone else?"

I stood up, which hurt a bit. I made a show of the pain to gain some sympathy. "Of course not," I said. "Do you think I would wait until *after* I had a heart attack to have an affair?"

"No, I think this has been going on for a while," she said, turning away. "The late nights with Frank. You were with someone else."

"Honey, you're being crazy."

She spun around to face me. "Then why are you being

so sneaky?"

"I'm not," I said, avoiding eye contact.

"Tell me the truth or else. I *know* you're having an affair."

My head dropped. The fifth amendment was not an option. I was stuck. "I—I've been doing a few things for Frank."

Nikki sighed, shook her head and turned her back. I reached out for her, but she shuffled further away. "I needed to catch up," I said. "I could lose my job—"

"They guaranteed you a spot," she shot back.

"Guarantees mean nothing anymore."

"I can't believe you would jeopardize your health like this," she said, tears beginning to fall. "So selfish!"

My attempts to pacify the situation quickly turned to anger. "Selfish? Selfish? I've done all of this for you! Do you think this is fun for me?"

"No, I think it's an obsession."

"You have no appreciation for what I do for you," I said.

"If you cared so much for me and your family, you would stop. All you needed to do was rest, to spend time with us. That, apparently, was too much."

"I can't take it!" I screamed. "I'm bored out of my mind!"

Nikki sneered. "I'm *so* sorry that your family bores you," she said, dripping with sarcasm. "Maybe if we were more like Frank."

She stormed out of the room. I let her blow off some steam, sneaking off one last email. Outside the room, I heard loud rustling. Curiosity took over and I followed the sounds to the bedroom. There Nikki was quickly packing bags.

"What are you doing?" I asked, watching her stuff her clothes into the suitcase.

"I'm taking the kids to my mom's," she said, ceasing packing to look me in the eye. "I can't be around this. You're destroying yourself."

I grabbed the bag out of her hand. "Stop being crazy," I said.

"I'm crazy if I stay and accept that you'll kill yourself," she said. "You need to see what life is like without a family to support. Let's see if Frank comes to your rescue."

"Do you feel threatened by Frank?" I asked.

"Yes I do," she said. "He's going to kill you if you continue living like this. You need to make a choice—your job or your family. Because you clearly can't handle *both*."

I threw the bag across the room. My arm ached, but the adrenaline cancelled out the pain. "Go ahead, leave!" I screamed, as she picked up the bag and walked downstairs. "You'll never appreciate what I do for you. I didn't see you turning down the crap I bought for you!"

Once I made it downstairs, she turned around before leaving and shot me a withering look. "If I'd known there were conditions attached, I would have returned it all. You're pathetic." Then she slammed the door shut.

I caught a view of myself in the window, which caused me to pick up one of the kitchen chairs and smash it through the back window. The glass sprayed all over the kitchen floor, reflecting tiny mirrors of my broken expression.

***

Waking up alone proved to be tortuous. I missed the laughing of my children, the rapid footsteps of my wife, the ultimate morning person. It was now quiet as a morgue.

I instinctively picked up the phone, minutes after opening my eyes. Jamie, the intern, answered with a cheerful greeting.

"Hi Jamie, can you tell Frank that I'll be in today?" I said.

As I walked into the office, my body ached, but I covered it up with a swift stride, exuding confidence. However, my face must have betrayed my illusion of control. Jamie grimaced when she saw me.

"Are you okay, Mr. Vedig?" she asked, looking concerned.

"Yes, why?" I replied.

"You look like you're in pain."

I waved off the suggestion and continued on to my office. Jamie called out to me. "Your office is…occupied," she said.

"Occupied by who?" I continued on my path, hearing laughter behind my office door. Roughly opening the door, I saw Dave behind my desk on the phone, twirling in the swivel chair. He let out a belly laugh before noticing my furious gaze, which cut his joy short.

"Kumar," he said. "I didn't know you were coming back."

I left the room, slamming the door shut, without saying a word. My gait slowed down noticeably and the walk to Frank's office seemed to take forever. The weakness in my body sucked out some of the fury that I hoped to release on Frank. By the time I reached his door, I felt like I'd just biked cross country. My knock was weak and timid. I tried once more, harder but still underwhelming. This time, Frank shouted for me to enter.

"Kumar!" he greeted me. "What a surprise. You look exhausted."

"I *am* exhausted," I said between gritted teeth. "I had to walk all the way here because I'm not allowed in my own office."

Frank furrowed his brow, trying to figure out what I was talking about. "Oh right, the office thing," he said after a slight pause. "Sorry about that. We needed to provide Dave with a workspace while you were out. I wasn't expecting you back so quickly."

"Well, here I am," I said, raising my hands.

"Great! We'll find Dave somewhere else."

"Why can't he go back to his old office?" I asked.

"Someone took his spot, so that's not an option," he said, sounding challenging.

"Did you promote Dave?"

"I wouldn't call it a promotion, exactly," he said. "He did surprise us with some good work. But I would call it more of a temporary help-out."

"Now that I'm back, you won't need his help anymore, right?" I asked, trying to sound intimidating despite my labored breathing.

Frank looked down at his desk. "We got swamped while you were away. I know it's not your fault with your health and everything, but it was probably the worse time for something like that to happen."

I noticed that Frank referred to my heart attack as a *thing*. In fact, he never asked me any specifics as to my condition.

"But I can just take over what Dave has done," I said. "You know me, I learn quick. And I'll put in as many hours as needed."

"I know that, and sure, you can take over," he said. "Some of it, anyway."

"Some?"

"The merger proved to be a bit more time consuming than we thought. I think it would be best if we had the two of you dividing up the Evetrin stuff and the investments."

"So me and Dave are working…together?"

"I'm afraid that's how it will have to go," he said. "Why don't you share the office with him. Just for a couple weeks until we can find Dave a new home."

"Share an office," I repeated, feeling even weaker.

"Just temporarily," he said, flashing that old grin. I also noticed for the first time that his teeth appeared fake. For some reason, his gleaming, capped teeth brought out all the caged emotions of sadness, loneliness, and inferiority.

And I lost it.

"Frank, I need this," I said through growing canals of tears.

Frank leaned back, looking uncomfortable at the outpouring of emotion in his office. As he'd said many times before, a place of business was not the place to show emotion. Maybe he didn't look off-put as much as uncomfortable because he was not used to seeing emotion. His world was long-ago reduced to stone cold logic and facts, leaving no room for emotions such as a grown man blubbering away like an infant on his solid oak desk that cost more than most make in a year.

He awkwardly pushed a box of tissues over to my side, making sure not to touch me. "What's going on, Kumar?" he said, his voice lowering to a whisper. "Remember, honesty."

"My family is gone. Everything is gone," I said. The tears flowed even harder. "This job is all I have left."

For the first time, Frank didn't have an instant quip to meet my statement. He looked like someone encountering a screaming baby for the first time, so far out of his comfort zone. I wouldn't have been surprised if, in that moment, he jumped out of his seat and rushed out of the room to escape his discomfort.

But he didn't leave. Instead he asked a dumb question. "Do you want her back?"

I nodded, unable to speak through my plugged-up nose. My answer clearly confused him. "Why would you want someone to come back if they rejected you?" he asked.

I snorted in deep, clearing my sinuses enough to speak. "Because she's everything to me."

"But you said that your job is all you have left," he replied.

"Yeah, because she left me—they left me."

"But you still have the job," he said, still looking confused. "There's plenty of people out in the world, but only very few get to be as successful as you are. Do you hear what I'm saying?"

"But I don't want anyone else!" I yelled, sending tears flying toward Frank, who jumped back as if it was molten lava. "I love *them*, not plenty of other people."

"Love is temporary, Kumar," Frank said, finally relaxing back to his comfort zone. "I've been married three times, so I would know. Each one of those marriages, I was deeply in love."

"It wasn't real love then," I replied.

Frank feigned insult. "Oh we all think we know what love is. Do you know I almost gave up the opportunity to be CEO when I was with my second wife?"

I cleaned the tears off my face. "Really?"

"True story," he said. "She wanted me to join her in Hungary, start a little tea shop. Sounds romantic, right? The problem was that I didn't want to do it. This was *her* dream, not mine. My dream was always to run a company like Green Point. I wanted to be in charge. You know why?"

"The power?"

"No, but I like that too. It was because I'm good at making decisions and I enjoy doing it. I couldn't make any sense of throwing away the one thing I liked doing, that I excelled at, for someone else's dream."

"But when you really love someone, it's not just about what *you* want. You should want to make them happy."

"I did want to make her happy," Frank said, lighting a cigar. I'd never seen him smoke in the office before. "But what made her happy had nothing to do with me. Going to Hungary and starting a tea shop was what made her happy. And she did end up doing it. And I paid for the whole thing."

"You paid for your ex-wife to move to another country and start a new life?"

"Of course!" he said with a bright smile. "What better way to get over a failed marriage than send them away. This is what I've been telling you about money. Money gives you choices."

"You moved on, just like that? How?"

"I don't let myself get attached. Ever," he said. "If that sounds so terrible, then think about this. Joanne, my second wife, got what made her happy. I got what made me happy. We both won."

"But you lost her," I added.

"I didn't lose her," he said. "I let her go. Couldn't be more different."

"What about Green Point? You're definitely attached to that."

"Oh, absolutely," he said. "I'll probably die the day I retire. Which I never plan to retire."

"Never?"

"Why would I voluntarily stop doing something that I love? Some people find their life's meaning in their children. I found my life's meaning right here. This job defines who I am."

"Hmm, I never thought of it that way."

"Most people don't," Frank said. "They look at me like I'm evil, just looking for money. And that's because I am!" Frank laughed. "But they neglect a disturbing truth. Everyone's greedy about something. You may crave attention, respect, money, freedom, whatever. This might be from your parents, your kids, your wife, boss, authorities, God. This is all very messy stuff, emotional stuff. I've simplified the process. I set an external goal that I can measurably reach. After all, how do we know, without a doubt, that someone loves us?"

"I think you *just* know," I replied.

"*Just knowing* never squared with me. Too abstract maybe. I prefer the simplicity of financial reports, stock prices, quantifiable phenomenon. I like to know where I stand." Frank smiled. "What are you thinking?"

"I'm not even sure," I said. "This is so much to think about."

"Let me ask you one question. This will help you think a bit more clearly," he said, taking a pause. "What defines you?"

"My family, of course," I spit.

"You're sure?"

"Absolutely."

"If I may ask, why did your wife leave?" he asked.

I paused. "Because she wanted me to give up my position."

"Do you want to rescind your VP position?"

"No, I don't," I said quickly.

"Are you sure?" he said, a bit sarcastically. "Because I've got Dave on the case. He's got something to prove after all."

"No, no, I need this job," I pleaded. My words surprised me, causing my mouth to snap shut.

Frank smiled. "So I'll ask you one more time. What defines you?"

"I need this job so they'll be proud of me."

"If that was the case, why are you fighting for your job and not them? Sometimes, two goals don't match with each other. Your job is the reason they left, yet you say it's the reason they'll come back? That's very confusing."

"I don't even know," I said, putting my head in my hands. "I'm just so lonely."

"Loneliness passes," he said. "Besides, like I said, there's lots of people out there to keep you company."

Frank looked something up on his computer. "But for the sake of confusing you further, why don't you send some flowers over there. Maybe some toys for the kids. It sounds like she's doing this as a test. This will show that you're still interested in them."

"Interested? That's quite the impersonal term," I said.

"Well, I'm an impersonal guy," Frank said. "I'll send them for you. I'll even pay for them. Just as an experiment."

"What are we testing?"

"To see if you can buy back their love. You'd be shocked to see how easy it is. What's your address?"

I'm not sure if Frank's words comforted or frightened me. But at least I'd stopped crying.

Chapter Eighteen

"The price of anything
is the amount of life you exchange for it."
–Henry David Thoreau

I must have made over fifty calls between Nikki's phone and her mother's home phone. The ringing was endless, never answered, until the sound of errant ringing danced around my head all day, a constant reminder of the rejection.

It was difficult to focus on my work while these thoughts carried on. My mind created fantastic scenarios of what Nikki and the kids were doing. I pictured her already finding a new man, a replacement, who was home every day at five to provide his new family with all the attention they required. My teeth were becoming ground down due to all the gnashing.

Four days after Frank sent the flowers, I received a package in the mail. "Return to sender," it read. I didn't bother opening it, instead tossing the package straight into the trash, which was overflowing due to my negligence over basic hygiene.

Waking up was a recurring nightmare. It was a robotic routine that I refused to allow to become interrupted by any feelings. I was afraid of letting my personal life interfere with my work. I noticed that Frank failed to ask me about any personal matters, as he was obviously uncomfortable with my breakdown in his office.

But I still had Shah to listen to me. I reminded myself

of this as I waited out the clock that Thursday, ready for a pity fest at Shah's, once my workday ended.

***

Shah looked even thinner when I returned that afternoon. He stayed in his seat as I entered, his breathing labored, the wrinkles on his forehead seemingly multiplied since we last met.

"How's it going old man," I said, trying to mask my pain as I sat on the couch.

He nodded. "Life is beautiful, as always," he said. But I detected a lack of genuinity in the comment, as if it were an automatic response. "How has life treated you? Or I should say, how are *you* treating your life?"

My fake smile dropped. "Not so good, to be honest."

"Is this about your boss…Fred?"

"Frank. And no, this time it has nothing to do with him. Nikki and the kids left."

Shah looked like he'd been physically struck by my words. "I'm very sorry to hear this, Kumar. She left because of something you did?"

"Something I *didn't* do is more like it. She found out I was working. She's doing it to teach me a lesson," I said sourly.

"What is the lesson?" I shrugged. He continued. "How will she teach you if you can't understand the lesson?"

"She said that I'm endangering myself."

"Are you?" he asked.

"No, I feel fine."

"I recall you using the same words just before your heart attack. That hardly sounds comforting."

"I didn't have a choice," I said. "Frank was already starting to replace me. Another week and I would have lost my office."

"Your office is important to you?"

"Not the office, but what it represents."

"Which is?" he asked.

"Responsibility. The fruits of my labor. I've worked at this for years. I'll be damned if I'm going to let my lousy heart ruin everything in a month."

"How long have you and Nikki been together?"

"We were high school sweethearts, so about almost twenty-four years," I said.

"You put twenty-four years into your relationship and let it crumble in a month."

My anger returned. "I didn't *let* anything happen. She chose to leave."

"But she left, presumably, because you were endangering yourself," Shah pointed out.

"So she says."

"How could you have remedied the situation?" he asked.

"I've been trying to call, but no one will answer," I said, shrugging my shoulders in defeat. "They returned my packages."

"I didn't ask how you planned to get her to return," he said. "I asked how you could have remedied her concerns."

"There's nothing I could have done. It was that or lose my job."

"Are you sure of this?" he asked, narrowing his eyes at me.

"Yes, I already told you that they were *replacing* me," I said, my voice gaining an edge.

"You are, again, letting fear dictate your actions. Your fear of being fired led you to dangerous behavior. It sounds like your wife was simply trying to protect you, to ensure that you would be around for the kids."

"But she isn't being realistic," I exclaimed.

"You had a heart attack, correct?"

"You know that," I said.

"It was real?"

"There's no way that pain wasn't real," I said, shaking my head.

"And your doctor stated that your heart attack was likely due to stress from work?" he asked.

"So he says."

"If he had blamed it on genetics, would you have believed him more?" he said. "It's you who are not being realistic, Kumar. This job almost, *literally*, killed you. Yet, rather than deal with this situation, you dove headfirst back into it, like a burnt man jumping back into the fire. Don't you find this a tad foolish?"

"I'm just trying to regain control over my life," I said, trying to figure out how to justify what I felt was the right thing to do.

"Yet, you're losing even more control," he said. "What's more important to you, Kumar? Your family or your job?"

"My family, of course," I replied.

"Then why would you sacrifice your family because of your job?"

"She *chose* to leave!" I shouted angrily.

"All this tells me is what you value, not what you love."

"And being without a job," I said.

"Do you believe no one else would hire you?" he asked.

"Is your opinion of yourself that low that you think only one company will express interest? You said you spent years developing your professional self to get to this point. This is a waste of time if Green Point is the only place that will offer you a job, no?"

"But I haven't proven myself in this position," I said.

"Prove to who?"

"To myself," I replied, pointing my thumb at my chest.

"And what would it take to finally prove that you are a good vice president?"

"Growth, I suppose," I said, thoughtfully. "Good relations with my employees."

"Interesting," he said, leaning forward in his chair. "Do you not feel you've experienced personal growth throughout this ordeal?"

"I wake up feeling half-alive every day," I said. "It's a battle to get out of bed and face the world. I'm afraid that the world will see me for what I am—a failure. So no, I don't feel like I've achieved growth. Quite the opposite, in fact."

"Why do you feel like a failure?" he asked.

"I let the job get the better of me," I admitted. "I ended up in the emergency room in under a year. What does that tell you?"

"Perhaps you weren't ready for the position," he said, leaning back in his chair waving his hand in the air, in front of his face. "Or maybe you were never meant for the position."

"I *know* that isn't true," I said.

"How do you know?" he asked. "Often, we sprint the final mile with a broken leg simply because we ran the first ten miles."

"What does that mean?" I leaned forward, trying to understand his point.

"Perhaps you're stubbornly sticking around your job *because* you put so much time in, not because you actually want to do it."

"That's true to a point," I said, relaxing and sitting back again. "It would be a wasted twenty years if I didn't keep moving forward."

"Was that all it was for? You gained nothing but an office?"

"No, but it was the reason why I stuck through it," I said. "The office was the pot of gold at the end of the rainbow."

Shah waved dismissively. "Pot of gold? At the end of the rainbow, you simply find more rainbow."

"So nothing is gained from hard work?" I questioned him.

"I didn't say that. You don't get the pot of gold, but you get to experience the beauty of the rainbow," he said. "That was the gift. You're so wrapped up in finding *the end* that you forgot to look at the rainbow."

"And what would *looking at the rainbow* entail?"

"Acknowledging that over this period of time, you built a beautiful family," he said. "You were able to attract a wife who loves you so much that she's willing to leave the thing she loves most in order to save you."

"Are you taking her side?" I accused.

"There are no sides," he said. "You are married, no?" Marriage is a union, meaning that you are connected. Sides only exist in your mind."

I sighed, indicating my concession to his point. I had nothing left. "The question now," I said, "is how do I get her back?"

"How should I know?" he said with a playful shrug.

"What do you mean?" I raised my voice, unappreciative of his nonchalance. "I came here to find out how to put my life back together."

"So I'm the gold at the end of the rainbow?" he asked. "You come to me for results? Funny, I just thought you enjoyed my company."

"I do," I said, settling down. "I didn't mean it like that. But I really need some advice."

"There's nothing you can do to *make* her come back. That's her decision to make."

"How can I influence her decision?" I asked, desperate for an answer.

"You can't, nor should you," he replied.

"What can I do?"

"Live your life," he said, in a matter-of-fact tone. "Meet new people. Enjoy the fact that you're breathing, like how you felt after the heart attack."

"I can't just make myself think something," he said.

"Sure you can," he said. "Remember when we meditated? You made your mind avoid thinking about your problems."

"That's fine temporarily, but when I came back, the problems were still there," I said.

"Meditating once won't make you a master," he said. "You spent twenty years preparing to be VP. You should know that mastery does not come easily."

"This is unbelievable!" I shouted. "My family leaves me, I'm in ruins and your solution is to meditate?"

"What's your other option?"

"Fight to get her back."

"And you believe this will work?" he said. "Your

wife's problem lies in your work life taking over. Yet you continue to work just as hard. It doesn't appear that you're fighting very hard, if that's the case."

"There's got to be a way to have both," I said.

"I'm afraid not, Kumar," he said, with a gentle shake of his head. "Not with the mental state you currently find yourself in."

"Sorry, but I expect her to support me in my decisions," I said.

"Yet you are not beholden to supporting her decisions?"

"Not when her decision is to leave me," I said.

"She clearly explained her reasoning and you chose to ignore it. That speaks loudly."

"And I just sit and wait for her to make a decision?"

"I didn't say that either," he said. "Live your life in the meantime, find something that will make you happy and occupy your troubled mind."

"I can't believe you're telling me to just let it go," I said in disbelief. "This is serious. This is my life."

"All the more reason why you should hold it sacred," Shah said.

"You know, you're just like Frank," I said. "You both tell me not to care." I stood and started to gather my things.

"This has nothing to do with not caring," he said. "You can sit around and torture yourself, call your wife and receive no answer. Or you can enjoy your life, try to better yourself and use this opportunity to figure out what you really want in life."

"I want my family back!"

Shah seemed to be fading the angrier I got. I started for the door and he called after me. "You can decide to control the uncontrollable or you can let the process unfold naturally. I would advise you to choose the latter, for your physical and mental health."

I turned around, wanting to give Shah one last verbal shot. "Let the process unfold naturally," I repeated. "I just figured something out. Your approach to everything is to do *nothing*. You are one of those types who waits for life rather than going out and getting it. This is why you sell hot dogs in the park. You're a lonely old man who's never done anything of significance. I don't know why I've been listening to you."

"You haven't been listening to me," he said, closing his eyes. "That is clear."

I moved in further, not yet done with my excoriation. "That's the difference between you and Frank. You sit back and watch life pass you by. When Frank sees something he wants, he goes and gets it, *aggressively*."

"And what happens when there's nothing left to want?" he asked, his eyes still closed.

"Then you've won," I said. "This is why Frank leads a Fortune 500 company and you struggle to sell street meat. You're a loser."

"You're treading a very dangerous path," he said, his eyes opening.

My goal was to anger him and I felt like I was succeeding. "What's the matter, you going to hit me?" I taunted.

"Never," he said. "You will destroy yourself further trying to swim against the current."

"Yeah, we'll see," I said with a mad grin. "You know what? Thank you for *inspiring* me. This talk today motivated me to be the *best* VP that company has ever seen. Once Frank's gone, I'll take over."

"Then you'll die too."

"I'll die powerful, rich, and happy."

"Bless you wherever you may find yourself," he said, closing his eyes again. His composure made me want to scream. I turned around and slammed my fist against the wall, then left.

Chapter Nineteen

"The best years of your life are the ones in which you decide your problems are your own. You do not blame them on your mother, the ecology, or the president. You realize that you control your own destiny."
—*Albert Ellis*

My focus over the next two weeks bordered on obsession. I fell into the habit of arriving at the office at dusk, never leaving before midnight. Some nights, I slept at my desk.

Conversation between Dave and I was infrequent. The day following the Shah incident, I sought to make our relationship clear when Dave attempted to ask about my weekend.

"I'm not interested in chit-chat," I said to him, resuming my work.

"We're just going to sit across from each other and not talk?" he said.

"Yes, that's exactly what's going to happen," I replied, refusing to look at him.

"Can I at least put on music?" he asked.

"No, I need quiet to get my work done."

And this went on for the rest of the week. Every movement made by Dave enraged me. To my delight, Dave requested a different office and was moved to the fifth floor. As far as I was concerned, I had won that battle.

I was alone again and glad for it. My mere presence sent my coworkers scattering, like I parted the seas as I stormed down the halls. If someone dared make eye contact, I simply sneered and their gaze redirected. I was powerful. I was feared. And I didn't care.

The only time I opened my mouth was to report my progress to Frank. He'd taken over the meetings, telling me that the investments were more important at the moment. I had progressed past the analytical stage and was now actively managing the investment portfolio. Numbers were my only friend. Numbers would never leave.

One day, during one of my manic check-ins with Frank, he sat me down. I expected him to praise my recent focus, perhaps even offer me a raise due to the outstanding decisions I'd made on behalf of the company.

What he ended up saying was surprising, in the least.

Frank stared at me, appearing to analyze my mood. "How are things going, Kumar?" It was unusual for Frank to inquire about my life.

"It's going great," I spat, rapid-fire. "I'm more focused than I've ever been. These deals are my life right now and I'm dedicated to seeing this through."

Frank winced at my reply. "Kumar, I'm going to level with you here," he said. "You don't look so good."

"How so?" I asked.

"You don't look like you're sleeping," he said. "Are you sleeping?"

"Like a baby," I lied. I was lucky if I got an uninterrupted three hours each night.

"You just look a bit...disheveled these days. Not yourself. Is it the family thing?" he asked, as if my family problems were equivalent to having car trouble.

"I'm over it, Frank," I said. "I feel more clear, more focused. I've decided to cut all that emotional stuff out of my life. This job is my life now."

Frank sighed. "Look kid, I'm happy to hear that you're so enthusiastic about Green Point. We certainly need that. But I'm a bit afraid that you're going to burn yourself out."

His concern confused me. I'd never seen this side of Frank. "Don't worry," I said. "Burnout happens to people who don't enjoy what they are doing. I can assure you that I love what I do."

"You love analyzing expense reports? Calculating debt to equity ratios?"

"I live for it sir," I said, passionately. "It puts me in my own little world."

"Hmm, so it's an escape for you?" he asked.

"You could say that," I said.

This confused him. "Call it what you may. I still see a problem. Kumar, everybody needs a hobby, something they love to do besides work. Like me; I love playing golf, going to the casino, stuff like that. This allows me to relax my brain a bit."

"I love my work," I insisted. "*That's* my hobby."

"But what changed? You were ready to jump off a building a few months ago. Now your family leaves and you say *this* is your love. Forgive me for seeing a connection between the two."

"Maybe it had a bit of…an impact," I said. "But I think it's more than that."

"Okay, well, this is going to be tough then." He stretched. My heart beat like a helicopter, causing my palms to fill with sweat. Frank continued. "I've received some complaints from other employees."

"Who was it?" I blurted. I ran through my mental rolodex of possible culprits. How dare they complain about me. I was taking initiative, completing the important work so this company could survive into the next decade. And this is how they repay me?

Frank waved his hands for me to calm down. "I can't tell who said it," he said. "It's not important. But I *can* tell you that it was more than one employee. It wasn't malicious. They're concerned about you, Kumar. *I'm* concerned about you, and that's saying something." Frank laughed to try and tamper down the tension, but I was in no mood for humor.

"I thought there's no emotion in business," I said sourly.

"You shouldn't be so literal," he said. "It's different if someone's safety is at risk. We're talking basic human decency here."

"I didn't know you possessed that," I spit.

Frank smiled. "I'll assume you're joking," he said. "But maybe you got the wrong idea of me."

"What do you mean by safety?" I asked.

"Well they're...concerned with your behavior. You stalk around here like a robot, with no regard for anyone. You know the times we live in are...complex, dangerous. People may be getting the wrong idea—"

"What, do you think I'm going to come in here and shoot the place up?" I said with a smirk.

"No one said that," Frank said, holding his heads up defensively. "That's going too far. But you *did* have a heart attack not that long ago. I think it's more that they don't want to walk in on you dead on the floor...neither do I."

I stared at the ceiling. "You created this monster, Frank," I said, returning to his gaze. "With all your talk of getting rid of emotions. That's exactly what I did. I focused on my work and that's it. What do I get for it? My co-workers think I'm a psycho."

"Again, I think you take my words a bit too literally," he said. "Life isn't black and white—emotion versus no emotion, love versus hate. There's a lot of gray in the world. Being too principled can drive a man mad."

"Then why did you say all that stuff about emotion?" I asked.

"Because I like to talk," he said. "I have no inner monologue. And it helps that you're a good listener… maybe too good. But I don't expect you to follow my every word. Hell, *I* don't believe half the crap that I say."

"So you mess up my mind, then just divorce yourself of the whole thing?" I said, my voice cracking. "That seems extremely irresponsible."

"It's irresponsible to blame someone else for your problems," he said.

"I've heard that before," I said sarcastically.

"Everything is a choice, Kumar." He sighed, readying himself for his main point. "That's why I'm *choosing* to make you take a vacation."

I burst forward in my chair. "Frank, no, you can't do—"

He held his hand out for me to stop. "Listen Kumar, you've worked hard. No one doubts that. But you need a mental vacation from all of this."

"This does *not* sound like you, Frank—"

"Oh, believe me, it's selfishness on my part," he said. "If you go off the deep end, you're not going to be very useful to Green Point, right?"

"But not right now," I said. "I need this—"

"No, you don't," he said, cutting me off. "You need a vacation. You've made a ton of money. Use it. Money isn't there to accumulate. It's to allow choice."

"I choose to stay here and work."

"That's not a choice," he said. "It's a crutch."

Tears streamed down my face. My hands shook with rage. I was trying to hold it together, trying not to lose my mind in front of Frank. Perhaps, accidentally, a bit of honesty spilled out when I said, "I can't be alone with my thoughts right now. *That* is what will kill me."

"That's something that you need to sort out Kumar," he said. "I'm no spiritual advisor or psychologist. I'm a capitalist. So, this is a bit outside my area of expertise."

"I can sort it out by keeping busy—working," I pleaded.

"And what happens when the work is done?" he asked. "Those thoughts will still haunt you. And they'll come raging back, believe me."

I stared at the floor, unable to speak. Finally, I nodded slowly. "Okay," I whispered.

Frank beamed. "Fantastic! This will be good for you kid."

***

The guilt from accosting Shah was eating me up, no matter how much I tried to convince myself that I didn't care. I decided to stop by the park and see him before I went home. Shah was cleaning his cart when I arrived, so focused on the task that he didn't see me sidle up.

"Can I get a hot dog before you close up?" I asked, softly.

He looked up and saw me, fortunately releasing a smile. "Hi Kumar. Settled down, I see," He went back to cleaning.

"Yeah, I'd say so," I said. "I wanted to apologize for how I acted. I was being crazy. It was just—"

"No need to apologize," he said. "You only need to try

harder. That's more than any apology."

"I've been thinking about what you said and I've been trying to put it into practice."

"And what have you been putting into practice?" he asked, still cleaning.

"I've been trying to disconnect a bit, be more focused on my work, less emotionally attached." I purposely ignored the scene in Frank's office, the complaints, the *safety* issue.

Shah sighed, then stood up. "Kumar, you're *again* misinterpreting what I'm saying," he said. "What you're talking about is nihilism, the complete dismissal of others. You're seeing disconnection as a virtue."

"Because connecting didn't do me any good," I explained. "Remember how I was acting last week?"

"You were acting that way because you weren't getting what you wanted, not because of too much connection."

I threw up my hands. "Then I give up. I don't understand what you or Frank are talking about I guess."

He moved in closer. "What you seek is joyful detachment, the erasing of needs, of pain. Instead, you're falling into a miserable detachment from other people, a hatred and resentment of others. Because they hurt you. Yet others will help you and heal you. But not if you're closed off. Don't think of people as possessions, but rather as extensions of yourself."

"But I should still leave Nikki alone?"

"That's up to you, I'm an old man not a marriage counselor." he said. "Remember, live life." He handed me a hot dog and a canister of mustard. "Now if you'll excuse me."

***

I ambled home, staring at the cracks in the concrete. How I wanted to disappear in them, to rid my life of those thoughts battling in my mind. My razor-sharp focus was now a television of constantly switching stations, with thoughts stopping in mid-sentences and restarting—an endless loop of garbled junk.

An email alert temporarily snapped me out of the stupor. It was a reminder for the Hawaii trip I booked several months ago as a surprise to my family. What had been designed as a last-ditch effort to save my family instead served as a reminder of what I lost.

Then, I remembered that I had a choice.

The tickets were paid for, non-refundable. It would have been a waste to not use them. Frank had *ordered* me to take a vacation after all. If anything, it would be insubordination to not go.

"I'm going to Hawaii," I whispered to myself.

It was then that I realized I didn't own a bathing suit.

Chapter Twenty

"Money never made a man happy yet, nor will it. The more a man has, the more he wants. Instead of filling a vacuum, it makes one."
–Benjamin Franklin

I packed my bags with the thoroughness of a safecracker. Once I'd read the email, I set out to create some order out of my life. My clothes dangled on doorknobs to where there was no available real estate left. Mail sat in piles, unopened on my kitchen table, which was covered in congealing stains of questionable origin.

Hours later, my clothes lay folded with military precision within my suitcase. Toiletries filled the side pockets in order of usage frequency. While I was at it, I tackled the kitchen, cleaning the countertops, as careful as a sculptor. When I finished, I took an admiring look at my handiwork.

The best part of the experience was the lack of thought. In performing such mundane tasks, I was able to *will* myself into Shah's aligned performance. I took this as an omen of what awaited me in Hawaii.

Fresh from uninterrupted sleep, I awoke early and indulged in eggs, sausage, and pancakes—a breakfast for a king. In the middle of feasting, the phone rang. Frank's number displayed on the caller ID. I answered with a jolly greeting.

My cheerfulness must have thrown off Frank, who stumbled on his words. "Kumar, what are you up to?"

"Getting ready for the big trip," I replied.

"Oh, where are you headed?"

"What do you mean?" I said. "Hawaii. We talked about this. Mandatory vacation, remember?"

"Oh yeah, yeah," he said absently. "That will be good." He paused over the line, breathing heavily.

"Did you call me for a reason, Frank?" I asked, supremely confused as to the point of the call.

"Yes, sorry," he said. "Kumar, you might...hear some things about the company...or me. I need you to try and avoid any negativity while you're out there. You know, with your mind state and all that."

"What is it?" I asked. The curiosity was eating me up.

"Oh, it's nothing," he said. "Just some old rivalries coming back to haunt me. All lies, trying to break me down. We'll talk about it when you get back. It'll be settled by then."

"Frank, you can't tease me like that," I said. "Is my job on the line?" The selfish questioning shocked myself. It was like Frank pulled me back toward solipsism.

"It's really not a good time to get into specifics," he said. "There's a lot of false allegations. I don't want to bring you into it at this point in your life." He paused. When he spoke again, Frank's voice gained an edge. "And your job is certainly not at risk."

"Okay, but I really wish you wouldn't dangle this carrot over my head like that," I said.

"Sorry, but I'd rather you hear it from me than anyone else...or the press."

"Press?" I exclaimed. "Frank, what is this?"

"Just in case it blows out of proportion. You know how things get. You send an offensive Tweet and next thing you know you're on the cover of Huffington Post. Society is full of vultures and the media feeds them."

His voice drifted off. I had never heard him sound so vulnerable. But the clock ticked and I needed to leave if I was to catch my flight. "Okay Frank, I'll stay away from the news," I said. "I haven't been keeping up with it anyway."

"You're better off that way," he said, sounding weary, like his actual seventy years of age. "Do me another favor and don't take any phone calls."

"None?"

"Well, no one from Green Point," he said. "Or anyone else who may try to contact you."

I wanted to inquire more, but my anxiety grew as the time passed. "Okay, okay Frank, I won't talk to anyone."

"Thanks Kumar," he said, leaving the words hang, as if he had more to say. I left him space and he continued. "While you're over there, live like it's the last day of your life, will you? Last favor."

"You got it Frank," I said. I hung up and dashed out the door to hail a cab.

***

With a rare ease of mind, I drifted away throughout the flight, failing to feel the usual anxiety I get during airline travel. I needed no Dramamine, no Tramadol, no alcohol. My mindstate was not of typical worry, but of acceptance, blankness. I was on my way.

The initial moments of my trip were awe-inducingly beautiful. I saw everything I'd turned away from in the previous months; the crystal-clear water, the soft sand, the gentle hiss of wind. I'd been refusing nature, removing myself from its reach.

While I waited for my flight, I registered myself for a barrage of thrill-seeking activities. Once in Hawaii, I filled the first four days with endless activity. I hiked to dormant volcanoes, went skydiving, zip-lining, scuba diving. Rather than sit around and torment myself, I threw myself completely into my days. My endorphins were running high from all the activity. On the fifth day in Hawaii, I'd run out of death-defying feats and decided to spend the day relaxing by the beach with a book.

After a refreshing swim, I retired to my hotel room. Then the problems began. With no obligations, no deadlines, no one leaning on me, I found it impossible to occupy myself. I sat on my bed, immobile, unable to make a decision. The speeding train of my life came to a stop and I had no idea how to start it back up.

I had forgotten how to live.

People went to bars, I figured. This is what normal, adjusted people did. The hotel contained a small bar downstairs, which was packed with tanned, smiling faces. I found a spot near the corner of the bar and planted myself in a chair. After ordering a drink, I pulled my phone out and logged online. The temptation to Google Frank's name ate me up, so I returned the phone to my pocket. The television played a news station, the breaking news scrolling across the bottom of the screen. I looked away, afraid for what I might see. I scanned the room for something to do, fortunately spotting a pinball machine. I bought another drink and proceeded to spend the next few hours mindlessly playing pinball, true paradise for a guy like me.

Hours passed, drinks were drunk. There were two mistakes I made that day. One was not drinking enough water or eating (so I guess that's two). Second was forgetting how low my tolerance was to alcohol.

The rest of the day ceased to exist.

***

I woke up the next morning with a buzzing headache, unsure of where I was. When my vision focused, I saw the glistening, white toilet and realized I was on the bathroom floor.

I checked my cell phone to make sure I hadn't drunkenly called Nikki. There were fourteen missed calls from Dave, along with two voicemails. I remembered the deal I'd made with Frank, so I shut my phone off and threw it in a drawer. However, before leaving I grabbed my phone, just in case.

After putting some clothes on, I made my way downstairs to get breakfast, but was hours late. The cleaning staff had just finished up as I reached the dining room. I got lunch in the bar, which also served food. Across from me sat a young woman with blonde highlights and a nose ring, who waved at me. I looked behind me, but turned back to see her approaching my spot.

"How are you feeling today?" she asked me, in familiar tone.

"I've felt better," I said, wondering who she was. "I'm sorry, but do I know you?"

She laughed, her face betraying any of the stressed lines of adulthood. "Sarah," she said. "We hung out all last night. I can't believe you don't remember anything."

"I'm sorry, but I'm not much of a drinker," I admitted, bashfully. "It doesn't agree with me as you can tell." I avoided eye contact, keeping my gaze on my BLT.

Sarah looked confused at my sudden shyness. "Well you were a lot of fun," she said.

I couldn't remember the last time someone described me as fun. We spent the rest of the day together, shuffling through the lively streets of Maui, sampling exotic fruits, passing quickly through the tourist traps.

Dusk approached and we found ourselves lying in lounge chairs, watching the sun expire. She looked over at me and smiled. I hadn't felt that content since the day I became Vice President.

Looking down at my hand, I noticed that my wedding ring was removed.

In a moment of weakness, I agreed to accompany Sarah back to her hotel room. Once inside, the tension grew. Sarah smiled nervously at me, then reached in to kiss me.

"I'll be right back," she said, moving toward the bathroom. The sting of her kiss still lingered.

My phone buzzed. I pulled it out to see that it was Nikki calling. My mind exploded as the room swam. Before anything advanced, I ran out of the room, praying that I hadn't told Sarah my room number.

Slamming the door quickly behind me, I hid in my room for the rest of the night. My flight left early the next morning, so I just hoped that I wouldn't run into Sarah in the meantime.

I checked Nikki's message, my hand quaking in fear. Her voice sounded sweet and comforting, just what I needed in that moment of mass confusion.

"Hi Kumar," Nikki said. "I know it's been awhile. I've been angry, but I don't think I need to tell you that. I noticed the Hawaii trip was supposed to be happening...I really hope you went. As angry as I am, I'm still in love with you and I want you to be happy. We all want *you* back. That's what is most aggravating about this situation. I know you're still in there." She began to add "I" but stopped. I convinced myself that she was trying to say "I love you," but who knows. She continued. "I just wanted you to hear that. You can call back if you'd like."

If I would like? There's nothing more I would have wanted. But I was so messed up, mentally, that it didn't seem fair for Nikki to hear me in this condition. I planned to call her first thing in the morning.

The next morning found me paranoid, too nervous to properly pack my luggage, which bulged so much that it looked like it might burst any second. I ran through the empty halls, my eyes closed, hoping Sarah didn't also have an early flight. Thankfully, I jumped in the cab without incident.

With ten minutes to board, I remembered to call Nikki. I absently held out my phone and hit the call button. When I looked down, I realized that I'd accidentally picked up a call from Dave. Unwilling to just hang up on him for fear that he'd know I was ducking his calls, I pressed the phone to my ear.

"Uh, hi Dave," I said.

"Kumar! Where have you been?" he said, panicked. "I've been calling you nonstop. It's crazy—"

"Dave, I really can't talk right now—"

"You have to hear this—"

"Sorry Dave, my flight..." Then I hung up. I was shaken by Dave's intensity. What was I returning to?

With thoughts swirling through my brain, I sat paralyzed on a bench until my flight was called. I had forgotten to call Nikki.

***

Once my taxi delivered me home, I rushed inside to call Nikki, who answered on the third ring, sounding exhausted.

"You took your time calling back," she said, the disappointment clear in her tone.

"I'm sorry, I was out of town," I said sheepishly.

"Where did you go?"

I paused, at first unwilling to admit I took the family vacation alone. The lingering guilt of the Sarah episode still held firm. But if I was to repair the relationship, I needed to start being honest. "I went to Maui," I said. "The tickets were non-refundable and—"

"That's great!" she said, sounding relieved. "I was hoping they wouldn't go to waste. How was it?"

"I had a good time," I said shakily, trying not to reveal any hint of what happened. So much for being honest. "I had a lot of time to think."

"Yeah, so have I," she said. "I'm not going to lie, Kumar. I miss you."

"I miss you too," I nearly yelled. "I miss you and the kids like crazy."

"They ask about you all the time," she said, sighing. "I'm afraid I might have made a mistake. This is incredibly confusing for them."

"Come home," I said, adding "Please."

"I—don't know," she said. "I'm just so afraid."

"Afraid of what?" I said. "We can't live in fear. We can fix whatever is broken. I'm ready."

"That's nice to hear," she said, not sounding entirely

convinced. "My opinion stands though. If we're going to make this work, you're going to need to find something else to do for work."

"Why?" I asked. Big mistake.

Her voice escalated quickly. "We've been over this, Kumar. Hell, you had a heart attack! That should have been enough of a warning. It's not going to work if you continue at Green Point."

I couldn't respond.

She continued. "Kumar, are you still there? What do you have to say?"

"I—I can't," I said, my voice fading. "Not right now. Once the project is over—"

"Always when the project is over," she said. "You're choosing your job over your family, Kumar."

I began to cry. "I'm sorry, but I can't."

"Then neither can I," she said before hanging up.

I needed to get my mind off this. Getting back to Green Point would relieve me of the guilt and keep my mind occupied.

Before setting out, curiosity edged me towards checking the voicemails left by Dave throughout the week.

I only needed to hear one. "Kumar, it's Dave. You need to call me back. Those investments that Frank had us on went south. I'm not sure of the full story, but it's bad stuff. I've been ducking calls from regulators all day. They're snooping around. Call me back, please."

This didn't sound good. I ignored Dave's request to call him back, afraid that our calls might be listened in on. The last thing I needed was more reason to be paranoid.

I decided to bypass the office for now and seek out some advice from Shah. If nothing else, he was always able to keep me focused.

***

I nearly crashed into a pedestrian as I was driving to Shah's. Jumping out of my car, I became winded by the time I reached his door. My body felt like it would collapse from the stress, but my determination to hear his voice kept me going.

I knocked three times, but didn't hear a sound behind the door. Holding my ear up to the door, I thought I heard light snoring. I pounded on the door, desperate for Shah to appear. After a few seconds, the door cracked open. I saw a brown eye peek out from the crevice.

"Shah, it's me," I whispered.

He let me in wordlessly and sat down, rubbing his eyes. "Where have you been?"

"I was in Hawaii," I said, looking around the room for any evidence of tampering due to my continued feeling of paranoia.

"You don't look like someone who just returned from Hawaii," he said. "Why so stressed?"

Sitting on the couch, I started to confide in him. "A co-worker left me a message saying something is going wrong with the investments. I was in charge of these—"

"I know about the investments," he said, holding his hand out for me to stop explaining.

"How?"

"You talk about them more than your family," he said. "These were ordered from Frank, yes?"

"Yeah, and they must have went bust."

"Frank was using them to enrich himself."

"How do you know?"

"I knew the very first time you told me about them," he said. "The secrecy, the sudden importance. The signs were all there."

"Thanks for telling me now," I said. "Hindsight is about as valuable as those investments."

"Why didn't you inquire about why they were so important to Frank?"

"I did ask him, several times," I said. "He said the company was expanding, changing directions."

"And did you look into this further?" he asked. "Perhaps asking the board for clarification? You are the VP after all."

"Well, no," I said, slightly embarrassed. "Frank is my superior. That would be going over his head."

"So you blindly followed Frank because he's your superior?"

"Not just that. I respected him."

"You respected his power, his material gains," Shah said. "This doesn't seem to be working too well for him now."

"I don't even know the full story," I said. "Maybe Dave was trying to keep me away. Do you think?"

"I think that Frank had a storm approaching for some time," he said. "He's one who let his personal pursuits trump the needs of the community. He'll pay for his mistakes like they all do. I suggest you move on with your life."

"What does that mean?" I asked, alarmed. "Do you think I'll lose my job?"

"I suggest you determine that by finding your mission," he said. "This position has caused you to throw away everything valuable in your life. For what?"

"Nothing…yet," I said. "It's the potential of where I'll be. I mean, if this is really bad for Frank, then maybe—"

"Maybe you'll take over?" Shah chuckled, lightly.

"Yes, why not me?" I said, offended.

"Why would you want to take over a mess like that?" he asked. "You will simply become Frank. It will only drive you further away from your family. Speaking of which, how is the situation with your family?"

I looked down. "We almost made up," I said. "Nikki gave me an ultimatum. The job or the family."

"And you chose?"

I paused. "You know what I chose."

"I need to hear you say it," he said, leaning in.

"I chose the job! Okay? I'm a horrible person, I get it."

"You're not a horrible person, Kumar," he said, patting my knee. "I don't enjoy spending my time with horrible people. You're simply making decisions on where you see more benefits in your life for now. But you're young. You have infinite opportunities to correct the situation. I find it interesting that you *again* mentioned the issues with Frank before talking about the troubles with your family."

My head was in my hands. "How did I get here?"

"You let your work define you," he said. "Your life became the job. Even worse, it was work you didn't enjoy. Remember what I asked you in our first meeting?"

"You've asked me a lot of things," I said, looking away.

"I think you remember."

I sighed. "You asked me about my mission."

"And what did you answer?"

"Look, I have a lot on my plate right now," I said. "I'd rather not—"

"What," he began, pausing to gasp for air. I noticed that his face grew whiter. "Did you say?" he finished.

Seeing him this frail state made drop my guard.

Compassion took over. I suddenly didn't want to be obstinate, to cause him further pain or frustration. I felt his love and wanted to reflect it back.

"I said that I always loved horses," I said.

"When is the last time you've seen a horse?"

"I don't know. Years," I said.

"Why?" he asked. "When you love them so much. There are horses around, no?"

"Yeah. I guess I got busy with the kids—"

"Kids usually love horses," he said. "Perhaps you could have passed on your passions to your little ones. What did you teach them instead?"

I stared at the wall. Everything fell into place. "I taught them that work is more important than family."

"Wouldn't it have been better to show them how to follow their mission?"

"Yes," I whispered. I looked him in the eye. "What did I do?"

"What's important is what you are *going* to do. The future eats you up because you *plan* to do things, yet you never take action to take back mental control over your life."

"How do I take back control?"

"After all our time together," he said, sitting back, "I think you know what you need to do."

Chapter Twenty-One

"Your life changes the moment you make a new,
congruent, and committed decision."
–Tony Robbins

After leaving Shah's, I drove around the city with no particular goal in mind. Part of me wanted to return to the office and find out the real story. I called Frank three times that day but got no response. Despite my curiosity, I was still repelled by the thought of calling Dave and allowing him to be my savior.

The flurry of thoughts dissipated as I ventured further outside the city. Surrounded by the thick groves of trees among the suburbs, I rolled down my windows and enjoyed the cooling breeze from outside. Soft music played on the radio, perhaps a Bach piece, that further soothed me into a blank state.

Before I knew it, I approached Kettle Moraine, about two hours outside the city. I wasn't sure of how I got there, as I couldn't recall the past hour. Yet I still had a huge smile on my face, so rare that it felt alien to my body.

I decided to pull off an exit and grab something to drink in Kettle Moraine. The town looked as though it was stuck in time; farm stands selling fresh vegetables, an adorable town square where old men sat on benches outside a general store, unmoving in the slow movement of their world. It was like I'd wandered into a 1950's sitcom.

I passed a sign that read "Eden's Ranch next left— Horse riding and more." Without thinking, I hooked the next left toward the ranch. The sudden decision frightened me. What was I doing? My life had become so meticulously planned that the mere thought of spontaneity gave me nervous chills of excitement. Yet, I kept moving forward towards the entrance of the ranch, where a refurbished red barn greeted me. I parked alongside and looked in the mirror. To my surprise, I was still smiling, looking like a total stranger.

Inside, the barn was illusively modern, with soft leather chairs spread out around the lobby. A gray-haired man with a slight limp approached me with a smile.

"Hello sir, can I help you? I'm Jerry," he said, offering a strong handshake.

"Yeah, I'm interested in riding one of the horses," I replied.

He chuckled. "Okay sounds good, as long as you don't mind messin' up your duds," he said, gesturing towards my clothes.

It then occurred to me that still I wore my work shirt and tie. More than likely, I looked like the most out-of-place person there. "It's fine," I said, loosening my tie. "They're just clothes."

"Indeed they are," he said with a wink. "What level would you consider yourself? Have you ridden before?"

"Not in a long time," I said. I couldn't even recall how many years had passed since I'd last ridden. The only clear memory I held was of my dad smiling from the side of the stable. He encouraged my early love of horses until the day of his death. Not coincidentally, I lost interest once he died, instead devoting myself to my college degree and losing myself in my studies.

Jerry helped me up on Daisy, a muscular mare who didn't seem too relaxed. "Are you sure she's okay?" I asked as I mounted the horse. My movements were stiff, unnatural enough to be painful. This might as well have been my first time.

Jerry laughed. "Oh yeah! Daisy is a bit of a worry wart, always moving around," he said. "You have to give her a bit of patience and she'll calm down. She likes it when you give her neck a little rub. Seems to calm her down."

Once on top of Daisy, the horse sidestepped, almost sending me sliding off her side, my body tightening. "I don't know about this," I said. "Maybe this was a mistake. It's been a long time."

"Too late now," Jerry said, laughing. "She likes you, I can tell. Don't be afraid. We miss out on the best experiences when we let fear take over."

"I think a broken neck is a reasonable fear," I said. My logical brain was taking over again.

Jerry laughed harder, coughing. "Aww, Daisy wouldn't do that to you," he said. "She bucks because she's testing you, seeing if you'll stick around."

"Why is she testing me?" I asked, my voice shaking from Daisy's undulations.

"She's had a rough history," he said, patting Daisy's back, which steadied her movements. "They all have. These are all rescue horses. They've been abandoned, abused, you name it. You can't blame them for being a bit...cautious."

I rubbed Daisy's neck, suddenly feeling compassion for the horse. My fingertips felt some sort of electricity flowing from me to the animal. The touch appeared to calm her, which put my own mind at ease.

"But the thing about these animals is, once you gain their trust, they're as loyal as anything on this earth. It's like the trauma strengthens them, if that makes any sense."

"It makes a lot of sense," I said.

Jerry threw up his hands. "Listen to me ramble," he said. "Let me get up on Livingston over here and we'll get moving." Livingston was Jerry's towering stallion, who watched Jerry's movements like a praetorian guard. For good reason, I aimed to avoid getting in Livingston's way.

I received some quick instructions from Jerry on how to handle Daisy and off we went through the forested grounds of the ranch.

About a mile in, I noticed Daisy's trot pick up the pace. I panicked, trying to pull on the reins like I was taught. "What do I do?" I yelled to Jerry, who was twenty feet behind, lost in his own world. "She won't stop!"

"You got to tug on the reins!" he yelled.

"I am tugging!" I said, showing him.

"You're not tugging hard enough," he said. "Give it a good pull."

"But it'll hurt her."

"It'll hurt worse when she sends you into a rock," he said.

The thought of bodily injury caused me to yank on the reins, slowing Daisy back down to a leisurely stroll. She didn't whimper or show any signs of pain.

Jerry rode up alongside. "Don't worry about hurting her," he said. "You're only trying to protect you both. It's more dangerous to let her run wild. The little sting is a signal for her to slow down. It's like a burnin' stove top. If you didn't feel pain, you would end up burnin' yourself. Sometimes pain is good." He picked up the pace and sped past, leaving me with the familiar words and the memory of Shah's first teaching.

An hour flew by like nothing. I became so enraptured

by the natural beauty of my surroundings, of the calm demeanor of the powerful animal transporting me. I forgot my issues with my family, my job, my life. My mind was elsewhere; calm, focused on the moment.

But sadness overtook me as I dismounted. I knew that I would have to return to the brutal reality of my present circumstances.

Jerry helped me off the horse as Daisy whinnied like she missed me already. "Did you enjoy that bud?" he asked me.

"That was...the nicest experience I've had in a long time."

"What do you do anyway?" he asked. "Sorry to intrude but I have to ask. Don't see too many come here in suits, you know what I mean?"

I laughed. "No problem," I said. "I work at Green Point as a VP. I was a sales guy before that."

"Whoa, a bigshot huh?"

"Some would say," I said, a frown overtaking me. "It's more like being on an out of control roller coaster."

"I hear that," he said, looking up, towards the sky. "I used to be a corporate guy myself. I couldn't hack it but I give all the credit in the world to you guys who can."

"Well, I wouldn't say that I'm exactly hacking it right now," I said. "It's caused a lot of problems in my life, with the schedule."

Jerry grunted in acknowledgement. "They'll take your whole life if you let them," he said. "Well, listen, if you ever need a change of pace, we sure could use a guy like you around here."

"Oh yeah?" I said, my interest piqued.

"Yup," he said. "I've got some good handlers around

here, but they haven't got what you would call *business* sense."

Through Jerry's slumped shoulders, I got a sense that I struck a nerve. "Everything okay with this place? Financially, I mean."

"Oh yeah, we'll survive," he said, betraying a tinge of sadness. "It's just tough getting funding these days with the economy the way it is. People don't like to think about living things suffering, so they ignore it. It's all kind of… perverse if you think about it."

"I'll say."

Jerry stared off into the landscape, then caught himself. "I'm sorry," he said. "Just rambling here. I don't mean to sound all depressing."

"I'll think about your offer," I said. "If things really go south with the job, I mean."

"Of course," Jerry said. "Enjoy yourself, where you're at. I'm sure you worked hard to get there. They need more honest folks like you in positions of power. That's the only way we're going to change things around here."

***

A smile lingered on my face for the entire ride back into the city. With my windows down, I felt the breeze brush softly on my hair and I remembered that I was alive.

The feeling subsided once I reached the Loop. Uneasiness took over, as my stomach twisted in knots, causing me to open the car door and gasp for air while at a traffic light. I couldn't understand why I felt this way. All I could think was that the stress of returning to work caused it. But this was my life. And Jerry encouraged me to enjoy myself, so it couldn't have been guilt. Yet, the feeling persisted all the way into the Green Point parking garage.

As I entered the main entrance door, everything appeared in slow motion. Bodies passed, blurs of energy zipping by, as if flecks of dust blowing around the room. I could focus on a few faces; haggard, tired, stressed. These faces were nothing I wanted to involve myself with.

At this instant, I wanted Shah. I wanted to tell him of the revelation I had that day. I wanted to tell him that he was right and that I was a stubborn child who refused to admit that I had created this mess. These misfortunes were not by chance. They were a culmination of my decisions, intended to strengthen my ego instead of strengthening my soul.

Yet, as these thoughts bombarded my head, I continued walking forward, automated. Still desiring to see Shah, I found myself enclosed in an elevator with a nervous man who impatiently tapped his finger on the metal railing.

"What's your name?" I asked, surprising both him and me.

He hesitated, then answered. "Um…Howard."

"Do you work here Howard?"

"Um, yeah," he replied, nervously.

"Do you like it?"

"Sure," he said.

"Do you know who I am?" I asked.

He laughed. "Yeah, you're Mr. Vedig."

"So you would naturally tell me that, that you liked your job?" I asked. "I want you to be honest."

Howard paused, started to speak, then recoiled. I nodded for him to continue. "It's a lot of pressure sometimes," he said, looking at the floor. "It's not you guys though," he added. "It's just…the demands of the job I guess."

I nodded. "Do you see your family often, Howard?"

He thought about it. "Not as much as I'd like, honestly."

"*Honestly*, I thought you would say that—"

Howard cut me off. "I'm not complaining. I'm really happy—"

I raised my hand for him to stop. "You should make it a point to spend more time with them," I said. "Your kids will grow up quick and that will be the biggest regret you'll ever have."

Howard laughed. "Well I want to, but it's not like I can just—"

"Yes, you can," I interrupted. "Don't let fear dictate your life."

The elevator dinged as the elevator car reached the fifth floor. "It's been a pleasure, Howard," I said, exiting the elevator.

My steps felt lighter, the carpet seemed to guide my steps along the hall. That grin returned as I realized the stomach pains were gone. I knocked on Frank's door, creating a little song out of the taps.

Frank spooked me as he ripped the door open, peering through the opening, his eyes darting around the halls, looking anxious, unusual. He waved me inside and I slipped through, nearly hit from behind as Frank slammed the door shut.

"Frank, I need—"

"No time for that, Kumar," Frank said, pacing around the room. "Things got bad while you were away. I'm sure you heard."

"You told me to ignore anyone from Green Point. So, I did."

Frank stopped pacing and stared at me, his eyes revealing a deep regret that I didn't think Frank was capable. "I'm ruined," he said.

I tried to spread my good cheer onto Frank. "Come on, Frank," I said. "I'm sure it's not that bad."

"It's worse than *that* bad," he said. "Those investments I had you working on—" he paused.

"Yes?" I said, stepping forward, urging him to continue.

He sighed. "They *claim* that I...was using them for my own profit...which is untrue," he said, leaning in for a response.

"Of course, Frank," I said mournfully.

"Why would I need them?" he asked nervously, seeming to address the entire room. "I'm already rich!" I've never heard a phrase like that spoken so depressingly.

Then a thought struck me. "Am I going to—" I stopped, unable to finish. *Jail*, I thought.

"I don't know what's going to happen," Frank said, dropping into his chair, then dropping his head onto his desk.

"Frank, why?"

"Do you know what happens when you have more than enough?" he asked, his face still on the desk. He didn't wait for a reply. "You want more," he finished.

I took a step forward to inspect Frank, to make sure he didn't need medical attention. On the desk, I noticed an envelope with my name on it.

"What's that envelope?" I asked.

Frank lifted his head and looked over to where I pointed. "Oh, someone brought that by earlier," he said tiredly. "Some kid." He passed the envelope to me. I tore it open, needing an escape from Frank's potential breakdown. The letter read:

To the Board of Directors,

As many of you know, the foundation of Green Point has always been the people and the goal for the company has been to create an environment of expression and personal and professional fulfillment. It has been part of the company culture and structure. The culture was created in alignment between corporate initiatives and personal fulfillment, this is aligned performance. Maximizing people for profit was the result of the aligned performance culture and it was at the core of the premise of the company's strategy for growth.

This is why Green Point has out-performed other companies over the years and has experienced double-digit growth. As of recent, it has seemed as though the company has lost this core value; the culture of the company has faced scrutiny and negative consequences because of this. You are the decision makers; however, my council is to remove anyone associated with this deal.

I tried to stop reading at that point, with little further need to continue. But I accidentally glanced at the closing:

Mr. S. Naahn

Shah?

I stormed out of the office, leaving Frank to wallow in his anguish.

Flying through the streets of Chicago, weaving in and out of lanes, I screamed into my windshield, feeling personally attacked, manipulated. Was Shah spying on me this entire time? He was certainly putting on an act with his wise old man stuff and now he knew all my secrets, all the work I'd done with the investments.

If I didn't take care of this, Shah would send me to jail.

I dashed up the stairs, two at a time, reaching the door with a jolt of adrenaline. Pounding on the door with my palms, I yelled out for Shah to appear.

A neighbor from across the hall emerged from his apartment. "Can I help you?" he asked impatiently. His voice, tone and the fear of arrest calmed me down.

I held up my hands. "No, it's cool," I said, suddenly realizing that I was caught haranguing an old man.

"He isn't around," the man said. "Ambulance took him away a few days ago." He re-entered his apartment before I could ask any more questions.

If Shah was in the hospital, then he couldn't have written the letter. But even if that were true, he still could have influenced the decision.

I left with a strange mixture of sadness and anger, genuinely sorry that Shah was sick, in the same situation I found myself a few months before, where Shah cared enough to show up. But the anger grew more prevalent, eating up any bits of compassion. Shah had ruined me, had taken away the one thing I had left.

The next two days were an extreme study in bitterness and solitude. Darkness blanketed the room, the blinds staying closed, as I sat pensively staring at a wall. I didn't want to call it depression, but there lacked any desire to talk to another human being. At that point, I would have been happy rotting away in that room.

***

I knew that I should have visited Shah in the hospital since he'd done the same for me. But the anger persisted, exploding anytime I pondered the idea of Shah.

Two days into my pity fest, the word *choice* stuck in my head and wouldn't let go. The word echoed in my mind, spoken by Shah, by Frank, by Nikki. It was a word I'd heard so many times over the past year that the meaning became so abstract, so elusive.

Then, I realized that I had the opportunity to *choose*. I had built up enough savings to last me the next couple of years, as long as I lived simply. I couldn't choose the circumstances that occurred: Nikki leaving, losing my job, losing a friend. But I could change how I handled these circumstances.

Sitting in a darkened room, staring at a wall was not a good way to handle the circumstances. My challenges were consistently met with anger, with blame. I had taken no responsibility over my actions, so I had refused to try and fix them.

And that's when it hit me. Shah was right about everything. I knew this now, I knew this before, but I was too stubborn to admit it. Wallowing would bring me no solace, but at least attempting to repair my burnt bridges would.

The first step was to get out of my filthy sweatpants and put some clothes on. I would attempt to see Shah, to communicate that I finally understood him. The poor, old guy probably didn't have much time left. It would be nice for him to know that his lectures weren't in vain.

In the midst of my sudden surge of motivation, my phone buzzed, shaking the kitchen table. I took a look and saw that it was Dave. My face lit up. Maybe I could make two repairs in one day, leaving the biggest, my family, to focus on.

"Dave!" I said cheerfully.

Perhaps it was too cheerful, based on Dave's awkward response. "Uh...hi," Dave said uneasily. "Is this Kumar?"

"Yes, of course it's me!"

"Kumar Vedig?"

"Dave, come on, you know it's me," I said.

"You just sound so...different," he said. *Happy*, he probably meant. Or manic.

"I feel different," I replied.

"Cool, because you're going to feel even more different after I tell you what happened," he said. "The board just fired me."

"Me too!" I replied ecstatically.

"You sound...happy about this," he said, sounding confused.

"Honestly, I could care less at this point," I said in a jolly sing-song.

"Oh, are you in one of those nothing-matters-to-me-anymore depressive episodes?" he asked.

"Far from it," I said. "I just had a realization about what's important to me."

"And a job isn't important?" he asked.

"*This* job isn't, no," I said. "In fact, it was possibly the most damaging thing that ever happened to me."

"And you're not worried about the Benjamin stuff? The investments? They're talking about criminal charges."

"Criminal charges?" I choked.

"Yeah, if I were you, I would lawyer up," he said.

"The last thing I want to do right now is talk to a lawyer."

"No, the last thing you want to do is go to jail," he corrected.

So much for ecstatic joy.

Dave continued. "But look man, I don't mean to depress you. Just wanted to give you a heads up," he said.

"I appreciate that," I said. "We should get together soon. We can talk about this stuff or just…you know…be friends."

He laughed. "I'd like that," he said, before ending the call.

Well, I had started to repair a friendship, but also found out that I might be going to jail. Call it even.

Chapter Twenty-Two

"Life is made of ever so many partings welded together."
–Charles Dickens

It seemed likely that Shah would be staying at Mercy Hospital since it was the closest to his apartment. Yet, when I rushed over to the hospital, no one could find any records relating to anyone with the last name of Naahn.

Next, I tried the University of Chicago Medicine, a larger hospital, which would mean that Shah's condition was more serious. But again, the lady at the information desk looked blankly at the computer, before shaking her head.

I started to think that Naahn wasn't Shah's real last name. What if he used a pseudonym to throw everyone off, to disguise the truth of who he was? After the letter from the board, I wondered constantly about the truth of Shah's identity.

***

The next morning, I received a call from Green Point's HR department. Karen, the HR representative, spoke robotically and impersonally, as if we'd never met. The memory of our brief conversations in the hall seemed to be wiped from her memory. Kumar, the VP, was dead.

"Mr. Vedig," she began, "I'm calling in response to certain organizational changes decided upon in the past week." She might as well have said, *I'm calling because you got canned.*

I let out an exhausted sigh to indicate that I was listening and let her continue.

"First off, let me issue the good news first," she said, sounding unlike someone about to deliver good news. "We would like to offer you a position in our sales department, effective immediately."

"Sales? Like where I came from?"

She paused. "Yes, admittedly it is a bit of a...lower position," she said. "But the position comes with full benefits, a 401K plan—"

"I know what it comes with," I said, tersely. "I've had this job before."

"Then do you accept, Mr. Vedig?"

I breathed heavily into the line. I wanted to say no, there was no doubt. But the thought of rebirth occurred to me, the ability to start over, to readdress my goals. Maybe I would take the position and use it for another purpose. The job would simply be a tool.

"Sure," I finally uttered tentatively.

I ended the call thinking that Shah hadn't ended my life, just derailed it. The anger subsided, but was replaced by a feeling of revenge. I would climb back to the top, in spite of him.

***

Being demoted was a harder task than I had anticipated. The work was dreadfully boring, which I had forgotten over time, with endless reams of leads and numerous cold calls with no results. I couldn't help but miss the feeling of making important decisions for the company, spending afternoons in Frank's office, hammering out proposals.

This, in contrast, was grunt work.

I also held myself in an aristocratic manner around my coworkers. I would work stories from my time as VP into our conversations, intending these mentions as important lessons to be learned, but really looking like a conceited blowhard. The days again crept by.

I lasted two days before I needed to take a mental health day. I took Friday off and treated myself to an extra-long weekend.

These were dark times, realizing my plans were foiled so quickly. I couldn't envision sticking with this for as much time as I would need to move up.

The next morning, I received a letter in the mail from Green Point. I half-hoped that it would be a termination letter, the news that my decision was made for me. But opening the letter, I discovered a somewhat cryptic message inside.

It read:

"If you love yourself, the world will love you back."-Shah Naahn

We request your service at the Antyesti of Shah Naahn as he transitions to the next stage. Services held at the Hindu Temple of Greater Chicago—Sunday, November 13

Rather than sadness or regret, the beast of anger erupted inside of me. I turned over my kitchen table, punched the refrigerator, anything to numb the anger swirling throughout my body. How could he leave so much unresolved? How could he allow our last days to be so full of deceit?

I bounced back and forth about attending the funeral. At first, I dismissed the idea, perfectly content to never see the man again. But I wanted to rid myself of these feelings, which would be less likely if I never got to unload this anger on someone. The anger was both my motivation and my mitigation, causing me to want to see him one last time and tell him how I felt about him at this moment. I never got the last word, the moment when I would make him realize his faults after spending so much time dwelling on mine. Why would I deny myself this right?

Chapter Twenty-Three
Present Day

"What seems to us as bitter trials are often blessings in disguise."
–Oscar Wilde

I drove to the temple in a blind rage. Traffic was worse than usual, more so as I approached the temple. More than once I considered turning around and heading back home, but the forward momentum of traffic kept me moving.

Upon parking, I made my way into the temple, where I eventually was confronted by Shah's son, as you know from the beginning of this story. After my brief, uncomfortable interaction with him, I felt out of place, like I'd made a mistake. I eyed the door, desiring to make a beeline out, no one noticing.

Without further hesitation, I dashed through a small break in the crowd. Making it almost all the way to the door, I accidentally bumped a man on the shoulder. When he looked at me, I almost fell to my knees.

I saw Shah's smile one more time in the face of his son, Jai. I must have looked horrified because his eyes expressed immediate concern. My body stiffened as I tried to look normal. "I'm so sorry," I said. "I didn't mean—" I couldn't even finish.

Then the smile returned. "No problem, my friend," he said. "You're the guy from earlier. I need to apologize about my behavior. You seem to have caught me in a bad moment. I'm a bit embarrassed."

"No worries," I said, my heartbeat slowing. "I'm a bit overwhelmed."

"Well, I'll ask you again, friendlier this time, how did you know my father?" he asked me.

"I became really close with him the past year," I said. "He had been giving me…well, lessons I guess. I'm not sure what you would call it."

"By any chance, are you Kumar?" he asked.

My eyes bulged in surprise, my heartbeat thumped. "Yes, I am! How do you know?"

"He mentioned you often," he said, offering a genuine smile. "We talked regularly. I'm stationed in Belgium, so I'm not able to come back to the states much, but we stayed in regular contact right up until the end. It sounded like he cared a great deal about you."

I felt a rush of pride, knowing that I meant enough to Shah for him to mention me to his son. Then I thought about the letter. If he cared for me, why would he essentially have me fired? As inappropriate a moment as this was, I couldn't help but wonder.

"It's funny," I said. "All the hours we spent together, he never mentioned anything about Green Point."

Jai laughed and shook his head, looking to the ceiling, as if addressing his father. "That's typical of him. He was always a bit embarrassed of his success. I don't think he ever *really* wanted to get rich. It just sort of happened to him. In fact, he found it quite a burden, having so much money to manage."

"So did he give it all away?" I asked.

Jai laughed again. "Oh, no." he said. "I mean, he gave lots away, but he was still filthy rich."

"Then why was he selling kebobs in the park?" I asked, really confused.

"He managed his money by making it work for him,

rather than working for it," Jai said. "He began to like money, in a healthy way, I mean. Money enabled him to have experiences. It enabled him buy the kebob cart and spend his days in the park."

"So he sold kebabs…just because?" I asked.

"His father, my grandfather, had a kebob stand back in India. Dad said in order to find where you're going, you must experience what your family has been through." Jai said. "I think it's what allowed him to live, as he would say, his *aligned* life. We thought he was crazy, me and my mom. But hey, best kebobs in the city!"

"Absolutely!" I said with a smile. I almost asked Jai why Shah had never mentioned having a son, but I thought this might not be the best time. Strangely, as if Jai could read my thoughts, he launched into the subject.

"In the early days, when things were really growing for Green Point, he worked a lot," Jai said, his face now gravely serious. "This is when I was young. He wasn't around much in those days. We had a few bad years. I went through my usual angry young man stuff, ended up running away to Europe. Luckily, that led to me finding what I wanted to do with my life."

"So that kind of worked out, in a weird way," I replied.

"Exactly as intended," he said, winking. "That's when I stopped blaming him. I realized that I *needed* this to happen. And so did he. This really bonded us together, this mutual suffering and redemption that we'd faced. We learned to love. Everything was better from then on."

"Is that when he quit Green Point?" I asked.

"Yes," he replied. "I found out quite later that he'd given it up, soon after I ran away. When I came back after ten years, imagine my surprise when my father, *Mr. Green Point*, was *selling kebobs* in the park. It was quite a sight!"

I laughed, picturing the scene. Jai shook my hand and excused himself.

I sat on a bench and played back Jai's story. Shah's story was my story. My horses would be Shah's hot dog cart—the humble symbol of freedom in a life torn up by chaos. Despite the overwhelming sadness of the situation, a warm feeling of calm washed over my body.

A tap on my shoulder woke me from my reveries. Dave stood, looking down at me with a huge grin.

I was shocked to see him. "Hey! How did you know—" I began.

"I'm a friend," he said. "We've been meeting up for the past year. The 'board'," he said, using finger quotes, "asked me to see him. Didn't even know he was the founder. Crazy, right?"

I laughed, entirely too hard for a funeral, but I couldn't resist exploding at the insanity of it all—these events happening concurrently. I tucked my head between my legs to muzzle the laughter, covering my mouth with my hands.

"What is it?" Dave asked.

I calmed myself, feeling red all over. "Just a bunch of weird stuff, that's all." I managed to spit out before dissolving again into laughing like a madman.

Dave look at me with a mix of amusement and concern. "You okay there, buddy?" he asked.

I looked up, my eyes wet from tears of laughter. "Better than okay, my friend."

"Okay then," he said, confused. "Talk to me outside for a minute. I got something to tell you, but I don't want to talk about it here."

Outside the temple, a few mourners smoked cigarettes, recounting memories of their time with Shah.

Dave leaned in excitedly. "Did you hear what happened to Frank?"

"No, what?"

"He was canned yesterday," he said. "The board issued the directive this morning."

"Is he going to be charged?" I asked nervously.

"Yeah, but Frank is pleading to a fine," he said. "Neither of us are implicated. Shah knew the whole story. I had been filling him in."

"So he was a spy?" I asked, raising my eyebrows.

He laughed. "No, he was protecting the legacy of his company," Dave said. "He probably let you go so you wouldn't get wrapped up in all this. Which leads me to my next bit of news."

"What is it?" I asked.

"They named me interim CEO," he said with a smile, trying to look humble. "I'm running the show, Kumar!"

At any other time, Dave's announcement would have sent me into hysterics. Instead, I felt warmth inside; happiness that Dave, humble, friendly, smart guy that he was, had been rewarded. "That's great Dave," I said. "Congratulations!"

"Look, I understand if you're pissed," he said, his smile fading. "You were technically higher ranked than me. And you put in the time, that's for sure. That's why I can't offer you your job back."

The statement confused me so much that I couldn't speak.

He continued. "Because I want to offer you a *better* position. I want you to run the company with me. I already talked to the board about it and they were…um, on board. Sorry, no pun intended."

I laughed, both because of Dave's terrible joke, but also from the absurdity of the situation. Dave had offered me my dream, the thing I'd dedicated over twenty years of my life towards. And I didn't feel all that excited about it.

Nikki came to mind. I thought about the long nights, the neglect, the anger, and realized that I had said goodbye to that life already. I held no desire to reacquaint. "I'm going to have to decline," I said.

Dave's eyes popped out in surprise. "What? Why? Kumar, we can be the kings!"

"I don't want to be a king anymore," I said. "I want to ride horses."

Dave had nothing to say as he looked at me like I had three heads.

"I'll call you next week. Trust me, I'm good," I said, patting him on the shoulder. I left him with his jaw still gaping open.

Chapter Twenty-Four

"Success is peace of mind which is a direct result of self-satisfaction in knowing you did your best to become the best you are capable of becoming."
                                                    –John R. Wooden

Three weeks floated by—filled with joy—as I began my new position, which proved both challenging and fulfilling. Every day, I acknowledged the blessing that I could spend my days in such a peaceful, supportive atmosphere. I had decided to use my money to help Jerry's ranch stay alive. I would visit at least once a week, riding horses, taking in the fresh, country air, using the ranch as my escape from the hectic week.

Sure, the commute wasn't great, but I planned to sell the house and move closer, trading my opulent home for something more modest. The house was too bare, contained too many demons, with too much room for one person.

Life without Nikki and the kids became more bearable when I was engaged in my daily activities. I found myself breezing through the acceptance stage, content with regular phone calls with the kids and the eventual decision of paternity rights, which we discussed briefly the week before.

One weekend, I invited Nikki to come by and bring the kids for a ride. We had been on good terms; cordial, not bitter, even when she revealed she was seeing someone. I didn't inquire, feeling like I didn't need to know. I was comfortable with the situation, accepting that this was how life would go from now on. And I would take any change gracefully, using each curious curveball to be a sign of my own progression, my own path to living aligned.

***

I saw the kids first, as they rushed through my office doors, instantly turning the serene environment into a tornado. I picked them up one at a time and spun them around, overjoyed at seeing their faces, which had aged so much in a month that it tore at my heart.

Nikki followed in a moment later, her steps tentative, nervous. She was clearly uneasy about coming here. I had thrown out a casual invite in our conversation a week earlier, mentioning how it would be great for the kids to learn how to ride.

We exchanged awkward hellos. Nikki told the kids to go explore. I told them to find Jerry to give them a ride, which sent them zooming out of the room before I could finish the sentence.

"You look good," Nikki said after the kids left.

"You look fantastic," I said. "I'm surprised you came."

"So this is your sanctuary," she said, looking around the grounds. "A little bit different, eh?"

"It's wonderful," I said, truthfully.

Nikki looked at me and raised her eyebrows, as if she wanted to say something.

"I'm sorry," she said finally, looking down. "For putting you through all of this."

"There's no need to be sorry," I said. "I should be thanking you, to be honest. I wouldn't have found myself if you hadn't left me."

"Funny how life works like that," she said, laughing

slightly. "I'm happy that you figured things out. It's hard to imagine that everything would have turned out okay like this."

"I don't think we ever imagined how things would actually be, and I've become more comfortable with it."

She nodded. "Me too,"

Outside, the kids' manic giggles filled the air, a sweet melody to guide us along the mystery of the future, the hope mixed with the realization that we would all struggle, but we would prevail. Shah had asked me how I would spend my last day on earth, but I was never able to answer. In that moment, I realized: *This was it.*

About the Author

Dr. Alok Trivedi is an expert in the field of performance. After building one of the largest health care clinics in the world seeing over 1200 patient visits a week he went on to become the President of Mental Toughness University. Mental Toughness' past clients include Coke, Proctor and Gamble, and Toyota and has been featured on media outlets worldwide from CNN, Good Morning America, and The Today Show. He has shared the stages with legends in the personal development industry ranging from Bob Proctor(from the movie The Secret), Brian Tracy, Don Yaeger, Steve Siebold and Grant Cardone.

He works with leaders and sales teams to create a high performance culture using a combination of processes that inspire teams to drive sales and increase profit.

Combining his expertise as a doctor and psychological performance, he has created the Aligned Performance Process. Aligned Performance is a behavior modification system using neurology and psychology to maximize performance.

The Aligned Performance Institute is dedicated to expanding human awareness and performance globally through media, audio, video products, live trainings and workshops.